Photo credit: Jaime Pimentel

After four novels, award-winning writer Merlinda Bobis returns to poetry. Her latest novel *Locust Girl, A Lovesong* received the 2016 Christina Stead Prize for Fiction and the Juan C. Laya Philippine National Book Award. Earlier she won various awards for her short story collection *White Turtle* and poetry, and her plays were performed internationally. About her creative process, she writes: 'Writing visits like grace. In an inspired moment we almost believe that anguish can be made bearable and injustice can be overturned, because they can be named. And if we're lucky, joy can even be multiplied so we may have reserves in the cupboard for the lean times.'

merlindabobis.com.au

Other books by Merlinda Bobis

Locust Girl: A Lovesong
(2015)

Fish-Hair Woman
(2012)

The Solemn Lantern Maker
(2008, 2009)

Banana Heart Summer
(2005, 2008)

Pag-uli, Pag-uwi, Homecoming
(2004)

White Turtle
*(*1999, 2013)

Summer was a Fast Train without Terminals
(1998)

Cantata of the Warrior Woman Daragang Magayon/
Kantada ng Babaing Mandirigma Daragang Magayon
(1993, 1997)

Ang Lipad ay Awit sa Apat na Hangin/
Flight is Song on Four Winds
(1990)

Rituals
(1990)

ACCIDENTS OF COMPOSITION

… there could be accidents of kindness here

MERLINDA BOBIS

First published by Spinifex Press, 2017

Spinifex Press Pty Ltd
PO Box 105
Mission Beach Qld 4852
Australia

women@spinifexpress.com.au
www.spinifexpress.com.au

Acknowledgements

Six of these 75 poems were originally published in the *Australian Book Review's* '2017 States of Poetry — ACT' and in the journal *Not Very Quiet*. Various poems were written during the 2016 Sun Yat-sen University International Writers' Residency assisted by artsACT.

Cover design: Deb Snibson
Cover photo: Merlinda Bobis
Typesetting: Helen Christie
Typeset in Adobe Caslon Pro
Printed by McPherson's Printing Group

National Library of Australia Cataloguing-in-Publication data:
Bobis, Merlinda C. (Merlinda Carullo), author.
Accidents of Composition / Merlinda Bobis

9781742199986 (paperback)
9781925581010 (ebook : epub)
9781742199993 (ebook : pdf)
9781925581003 (ebook : Kindle)

Australian poetry — 21st Century.

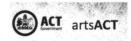

CONTENTS

Between a wish and a need:
a wish for a poem
a need to tell a story.

NOT QUITE STILL

AFTER THE GRAND CANYON

It's an accident
of composition: sun, sky, bird.
White orb on storm grey
punctuated by a raven —
but which composes which
and which is accidental?
Is it the sun
a hole
sucking in a bird
or Icarus about
to singe the sun?
Against the grey
soft and sinister,
anything is possible.
Look: barely a thumbspan
between
sun and bird
before the answer is given,
enough to fit
the fingerprint of god.

LUCY AFLOAT

After the scattering of ashes
Pulpit Rock, Blue Mountains

And then the light
on these layers of grief,
grit, glow
that make a rock.

From blinding white
to ochre soft, then rust
and pink running
into each other —
who knows which colour came first
or if the glow came
before the grit
before the grief?

Not even the rock knows
the secrets of its chronology.

It is we who look
who think we know
or wish to know
as we stand on it
to steady our feet,
steady our own running
into each other
and into grief
or grit
or glow.

MOTHER MOUNTAIN

Karst mountains, Yangshuo

You make we want
to kneel, to pray
even if I have tucked away
all the prayings of my childhood
in a box misplaced somewhere.

O arc of your crown
of green hair, fringe hiding
limestone brow lined
by water, wind, sun, maybe
even storms and all our years

of looking —
eyes have a way
of wearying those looked at:
awe, obeisance, even joy
are a burden of their own

even from a child
in love with her mother —
and you have your own children,
one cleaved to your cheek,
the others hovering,

eternally unweaned
as we all are
at your feet looking up,
returning to rock, earth, green,
beseeching you:

look back,
look kindly
on us, even if we have not been
kind, even if we barely look
back at our wayward tracks.

My prayer,
small, inept.
At your feet, the bamboos bow,
sway, lift limbs and leaves —
theirs, the truer prayer.

DREAM OF CLOVES

Perhaps at twelve, Fernão de Magalhães
dreamt of cloves. *Brown gold*,
he heard it whispered in 1492
at Queen Leonora's court.
So each night, as Page Fernão
closed his eyes,
a perfect earlobe hovered
above his bed, like a sacred reliquary
peeking from a braid of hair
and studded with a shimmer
darker than amber,
deeper than cat's eyes.

Within his reach,
how pale the lobe
pierced by this brown jewel,
this rare clavus — how still
this first dream that bloomed
into a whole ear
like a most fragrant flower
closing in on him,
close enough to whisper into:
Brown gold, he'd say,
the way His Majesty did
to his Queen, voice low
and full of import, lips almost
kissing her ear, her braid of hair
a-quiver with his breath.

But thirst stunned the boy,
parched his throat, his tongue.
Before Fernão could open his mouth,
the perfect ear rose
to the ceiling, winged now,
an ear-bird with a radiant eye,
this most precious find across vast oceans,
this brown gold that grew on trees
at the other side of the world,
this dream of kings, of mariners, of cooks.
Perhaps, Fernão missed
his chance each night
to pluck it free
from that wayward ear
teasing him to dream of conquests,

when all that the boy desired
was to flavour his sopa de lentilha.

AUGURIES OF A FISH

Perhaps it pans the room.
Perhaps it sees, all in order
not accidental but deliberate,
precise: Adelma hovering
among jars of azeite de oliva.

The virgin one,
the fruity one,
the lighter one?

There are choices here,
her one hand on the blade,
the other on her belly
howling back to Cape Verde
where she was chosen

because she was a little
lighter than her sisters
and she can cook.

Traders make good choices,
so did the Portuguese
captain who herded her
and fifty others to his ship —
then the endless Atlantic.

The virgin one,
the fruity one,
the lighter one?

She picks the perfect
olive oil for the cod,
its gills opening shutting
on the kitchen table.
Master wants it fresh,

wants the first pick
of this fiel amigo,
this faithful friend

or soon to be.
When all is said and done,
head in the pot for stock,
body filleted, spread out
and salted, indeed how faithful

it will be to the palate
of the Queen Leonora,
lover of bacalhau com natas
(and of her King, of course).

Again, her belly kicks.
Again, she hears it howl
all the way to her home in Cape Verde

and the memory of metal
around her ankles,
and a hand checking her teeth, breasts,
between her legs, lingering there
before the price was paid.

The virgin one,
the fruity one,
the lighter one?

On the kitchen table,
it hears the questions in her head
between trader and captain.
Again it pans the room,
then rests on the blade

just as Page Fernão
rushes in to report
that Queen Leonora has changed

her mind. There are choices here:
not cataplana de marisco
but sopa de lentilha with
a dash of clove, please.
The boy is polite,

well mannered, bright
as the stars he studies
each night, as he navigates

his books, his dreams.
Adelma, the new cook, nods,
pressing her belly,
Hush my little one,
and gripping the blade.

Again it pans the room and stops:
eye of fish locks with eye of boy.
This cod has always known.

This is where it begins and ends:
in the kitchen, the port
of all hungers, all thirsts.
But dreamers never dock,
so the gaze of Page Fernão

moves on, arrested
by the blade, the swerve,
the splatter of blood,
the final thrash of tail,
the petrifying of the eye

now locking in the boy again, in death:

on the other side of the world,
Fernão, you too will be gutted
by the namesake of a fish.

BALLAD OF THE LOST FISHES

En route the South China Sea

Where's the way to the reef? the tuna asks the grouper.
Where's the reef? the grouper asks the sardine.
Where's us? the reef asks.

The sea is quiet. It has lost its way.

Where are the fishes? the fisherman asks his son.
Where's the sea? the son asks his mother.
Where's us? the mother asks.

The sea is quiet. It has become land.

Where's us? again the mothers ask the fathers
ask the sons ask the daughters
as the last fishes stare

at all mothers fathers sons daughters

lost on land and laid on a plate, still
and staring back at them,
like them, once,

eyes wide open with no one to close them.

FEATHER, SEAHORSE AND ATOMIC EXPLOSION

For Dai Fan, Cloud Woman

On cobalt blue,
a white feather, oh
how soft against
Iowa's sky.
Afloat, fallen
from a tern
en route to the other
side of the world.

Then a seahorse
glowing peach
swallowed the late
sun in Mornington,
so a wary moon
pretends it's only
a toenail adrift
on grainy blue.

Now a huge white-
grey devouring
the sky turning
indigo in Denver,
aftermath of the atom
bomb over silhouette
of pines, sentinels
or charred remains.

Your triptych of clouds. I see them in your photographs captioned
feather, seahorse, atomic explosion sighted across continents.

I see them and see more. Such is the passage
from eyes to eyes, an evolution.

And the sky
looks back at us
seeking signs
we wish to see
from whatever ground
holds us, shapes us:

sometimes feather soft
loyal as a seahorse
malignant like
the atom bomb.

But in the driest season
it's the same
for us and clouds,
always
the evolution
of a wish
for rain
new grass
and maybe
even flowers.

15

THE FLOWERS THAT WOULD NOT OPEN

The mute child went to the doctor, because the flowers would not open. The doctor listened to his heart and sent him home. So the child returned to the flowers, tended them until he was a grown man. Still, the flowers would not open. One night, as an old man with an ailing heart, he visited the closed buds but tripped and fell. The buds quivered at the touch of his lips, at the last beat of his heart. *Tierra* הַאֲדָמָה *lupâ* أرض *föld whenua jörð bamal budongo* 地 *earth* ... it said in all tongues. And the flowers remembered how to open.

NEVER

Never, never speak to me
in the tongue of little roses.
Each petal hurts
because I live in white noise.
Each petal kills —
how red the wound
against the white. How fatal.

CALLE VERDE

Verde que te quiero verde.
— *Romance Sonámbulo,* Federico Garcia Lorca

Suddenly shadows
after the noonday glare
and you look up
and understand

why the suddenness
why the shadows
after so much sun —
look, a green canopy

of Bignonia Rosa
almost from end
to end of a narrow
calle — called Verde?

So your heart
contracts, narrow
now as your breath
caught again

by the ghost of a poet
looming *Green, green,*
I love you green,
chasing you all

the way from Granada
to Seville, and here
you slip out
of your skin

to *Verde carne*,
your hair growing
Pelo verde —
how this green

from waiting
for the dead
grown over and over
by moss, by age

yet longing to return
to his gitana
now long dead
from waiting,

her skin green-hued
by all the love years
lost: their green wind
still bristling

the sour agaves,
the hint of mint
and sweet basil
still sneaking

into your tongue
thick with old
earth — but then
a cat purrs

from a window
or so you think
and you are returned
to this alley

of trumpet blooms
and *Green, green,*
I love you green
slips out

of the shadows
and becomes
this Verde dripping
pink and lilac

and light dappling
the shadowed
cobblestones
that sing,

Un momento, por favor,
ahora es la hora
de la hora —
so listen, poet,

to what is growing
in the hour of the hour
lest you miss
the music.

STILL LIFE

For Yanfen and Guanwen

Eyes closed, cheek resting on his old rose shirt,
perhaps posed just so by the eye romancing
the newlyweds. *Hold it there, and hold her*,
it must have said, so his arm wrapped around
her shoulder, drew her close, and her cheek
found his heartbeat. Thus the hint of a smile,
as if she'd found out the secret of the peonies
on her dress, dark green of the Pearl River,
silk on her thigh, under her hand on her lap,
fingers slightly parted, making tiny causeways
for water or leaves. She sits still, but she flows.

Perched on the arm of her chair, his pose hints
slight tension. *Turn towards her some more*,
the eye must have said, so he twisted from
the waist up and the old rose creased, folds
repeating the arc of his ribs, and he must have
thought, but she is none of these. Whatever other
Adams fancy, she is not of mine. She is her own
arc, a river. And so he turned some more
to meet her, his own cheek suddenly resting
on her crown, his eyes closing, listening
to her dream. How still now, these lovers.

Against the grey wall behind them, for all time
they affirm, here we are: still life, still love.

THE IMPERTINENCE OF DAFFODILS AND BIRDS

She goes by the book,
she's scarily punctual,
she even makes appointments
for a cuddle, her arms trim,
sculpted for desire
like that Rodin arching her back
when she does stretches
at the gym — such exquisite
muscularity of the upper arm
rippling into shoulder
is no accident of gesture.

> The gardener from the suburbs,
> the au pair studying English
> and the cook imported from India know
> accidents happen only in other parts of the world.

Sometimes her spouse's eyes
stalk the ripple with
ode by ode that's never
written — there are accounts
to right, contracts to close
and words are not made flesh.
Tonight in Canberra, it's pillow talk,
her latest joust with the press,
his sticky deal with China,
and the bed dreams of Tieguanyin,
oolong blessed by the Goddess of Mercy.

> Yesterday, the gardener trimmed the hedge,
> the au pair did three sets of laundry
> and the cook learned how to be merciful
> to crabs — don't kill, just let them sleep in the freezer.

But the morning after, there are birds.
Only early August and there are birds
racketing on the hedge — or its remains?
She thinks, surely he cleaned up after.
Her spouse thinks, are those damned windows shut,
what useless double glazing. Downstairs,
a girl lights incense for Guanyin,
opens her little English dictionary
in search for the meaning
of *glazing* but finds only *glaze*:
cover, coat, finish.

    The gardener finished tidying the driveway too.
    O such delight — daffodils too early
    among the weeds — O such grief — pulling them out
    to recompose the order of the world.

AFTER REMING

Supertyphoon, Philippines
November 2006

Purple.
Unlike any that I've seen,
Mother says.
Behind an iron gate
beside an immense hole
on the ground,
but no house.

She pauses,
and I'm suddenly
beside the purple
behind the gate
in the hole
in the house,
led by the definite article,
thus definitively placed.

It is no accident,
this urge of composition,
as in the writing
of a poem
when I compose myself
into the loss of strangers
as if there was this hole,
this space reserved for me.

Around it,
the presuming poet builds:
it's the purple of bruises
after the boulders
the purple of the drowned
after the mudflow
the purple of death

after the storm conspired
with the surge from the Pacific
the lahar from the volcano
after the earth became
a whirlpool
that smelt of sulphur.
So I fill the hole,

I frame it,
lay out the scene,
line by line,
body by body
in that disappeared house:
a father, a mother, a daughter, a son
turning purple underground —

but I am halted,
as Mother resumes
her awe. *A purple*
hibiscus, a new bud
behind a gate beside a hole
that used to be a house.
Her whisper is deep,
unreachable.

Then she returns,
frames me in the evening light.
I doubt if you'd believe it,
you were not here.
Again she pauses and smiles,
But I'm glad you had a safe
trip from Australia.

THE LOST NOTEBOOK

He found it.
Ballpoint ink weeping
on the cover page
but still readable:
English Composition.

But inside
it's waterlogged,
unfinished. Only
the notebook knows
Nenita's final gift —

Reming, Reming
Shut your eye
Shut your mouth

An incantation
found in the hole
that used to be a house.

A poem
still composing itself
a week after the storm.

Like him now
walking round and round
the hole — composing limbs,
faces of his wife Gloria
and Roberto, fourteen
Nenita, twelve

like when he
composed himself
at work in LA,
composed his ear
locked to his iPhone

to the howl
of rain and wind
as he listened to
his daughter say, *Ay, Papa* —
before the line was cut.

CASSANDRA AFTER HAIYAN

For Cassandra Fate B. Merin, 10 years old

Your composition: a Christmas tree
with stick figures holding hands.
Your caption: *Gusto ko sama-sama kaming pamilya.*
(I wish we were together as a family.)
Drawn in crayons and labelled *First*:
first light after the storm
first sight after the dark.
Two-dimensional on Manila paper, a still
born from the frequency of storms.
But there are movements,
other dimensions.

What clarity of vision, Cassandra.

You round up your wish,
guide our eyes towards
its logic in the next frame:
stick figure named *Papa*
at the foot of a ladder raised
hinged to the wind
and at the top rung
a bucket unfurling a rope
tied to a foot vanishing
into the water labelled *dagat*, ocean.
How efficient: Papa, ladder, bucket, rope.

How simple your mechanics of salvation.

Then above his head,
another Christmas tree, now an arrow
guiding the eye to a house with two figures:
Bunsô0, youngest, and *Mama*.
Lest we forget: salvation is completed
in a house. But the eye unwittingly
moves to the next house.
Paaralan: School.
Inside, three figures also named,
lest we miss them: *Áte*, Sister.
Kúya, Brother. *Áte*, Sister.

What wisdom in testimony.

No child is safe without
a family a house a school.
Such is your eye for detail — the logic
of your first sight:
a Christmas tree with stick figures
holding hands — I wish we were together
as a family. We look at them
but do not feel the grip
of flesh, the stronghold
of a wish. It's just paper,
a child's drawing.

So who believes Cassandra?

Haiyan: landfall, 8 November 2013.
March 2016: more than a hundred
children still living
in transitional shelters,
the pledge of permanent housing
composed and re-composed
month after month,
storm after storm as
Cassandra turns her sight
away from the rationed crayons
and looks in the eye

another incoming landfall.

THE PERFECT ORCHID

To the women of the volcano

Is it the vanda,
waling-waling or cattleya
that's *the perfect orchid*?
Mother is in awe.
I follow her gaze:
such cool aristocrats
hanging way above
the soil, afraid
to descend.

But they descended
once, from the volcano
(livelihood of women
on its slopes)
to the stalls of women
at its foot.

Buy my orchids, Ma'am.

A year after Reming pushed
the ash, the boulders down,
they're back at their stalls:
Marlene, Gloria, Phoebe
who dug up their
buried houses.
Maricel who lost
her children
to the mudflow.

Look, a perfect orchid, Ma'am.

Mother checks it:
perfect petals, perfect heart
so still, so still
as if from a factory of silk flowers.
So, a reverent touch
to make sure it's real,
and the purchase is sealed.

I watch Marlene's hands
count the change.
Hands that dug up a house,
sure and survivor
perfect.

MUSINGS OF A CALF WITH A MOUNTAIN

Legazpi, Philippines. 16 November 2005

See, I'm nothing less
than postcard pretty,
an accident of composition.
I happen to have turned
around these banana trees
for a lustier feed,
and there you are
freezing me
with such intent,
even if I'm not yet ready
for the slaughter or the yoke.

So here we are
nothing less
than right for the taking
amidst this verdant idyll
right-smack in the middle of the city:
a little farm on public land.
Banana trees, a patch of cassava and sweet potatoes,
and among the foliage greener than your dreams,
a coconut or two
as young as adolescent me
flicking my tail this way and that —
and oh behind us, *her* of course,
the nearly perfect cone
ogled at and taken
again and again.

We are postcard pretty
with her serene and cloudless,
perfect through your lens
(and we the frame, the foil or frippery).
Good thing, old Pay Nito
who raised me from my mother's breast
did not follow me around these bananas
from his makeshift hut hidden by these trees
greener than your dreams.
His dreams are makeshift too
like the laundry hung from tree to tree
his blue blanket
nothing less
than perfect accent
for your rural composition in a city.

We are postcard pretty
fringe dwellers,
we are contraband:
this farm untitled, his hut unregistered
like him, non-existent
in the city books.
But *she* knows,
she knows us, yes she does.
Three years ago
we were on *her*, I mean,
the farm was on her slope,
my mother too
and old Pay Nito
younger then with a wife, a son,
a hut unhidden,

until she could no longer
bear perfection.
See, her mouth is chipped
against the sky —
old Pay Nito's ancient (real) wife.
Wedded still: farmer and volcano
and so I'm here,
grazing at her foot,
like Pay Nito in his hut empty still
since the burning
river from her mouth.

Take us then,
for we are postcard pretty.

JUNIPER SWADDLING

On Grand Canyon

How quietly
you sleep,
tucked
into the red mud
roof of a Navajo
sweat lodge.

And yet
I hear the swirl
of your mother trunk
in the way you're turned
just so —
in mid-dream
of sky and rock.

Were you her favourite limb,
once the top lookout
on a precipice?
Or the roost
of a Western Bluebird
that strayed too far?

How quietly
you sleep,
yet I hear
its love call
in how you're turned
just so —
as if to listen

between dream
and waking,
almost like
a heart.

WHAT OF EARTH OF SKY

What of earth, madam?
What of sky, sir?
And in between
your word
unworded?

Such is the poverty
of awe. Breath
began but never
finished, because
the pull of crimson
beneath your feet
the rush of indigo
above your head
are pull-and-rush unimpeded.

It's blood before your blood.
It's dusk beyond your dusk.

DREAM OF BLOOD

Blood courses through our language.
— Michael Rigsby, MD

*If I feel physically as if the top of my head
were taken off, I know that is poetry.*
— Emily Dickinson

Grandma's velvet buttons
or the petals of her reddest rose:
corpuscles strewn

from the top
of my head,
as if some secret

has exploded there
when you finally
arrive,

sneaky little thing,
you the glorious
accident.

By chance
you found me
or the page

in penury and starkly
naked — no,
you can't have this,

so you do
your sneaky
little thing:

settle in
and bloom
into a phrase,

a line, some
hothouse rose
or the bodice

of a red dress
I have yet to finish
sewing.

DREAMS OF A BOOKSTORE CAT

Only at certain times, the curtain of the pupils
lifts, quietly —. An image enters in,
rushes down through the tensed, arrested muscles,
plunges into the heart and is gone.
— *The Panther,* Rainer Maria Rilke

Are you dreaming of Rilke in Chinese?
Perhaps of your black and bigger cousin
pacing the cage of his poem
in Guangzhou? Or of Blake's striped feline
burning bright between your brow
slightly quizzical even in slumber?

Your head rests on a blue book, pale
and clear before the endless skyscrapers.
Your paw hugs a pile of deep
red, blood contained from spilling.
Your tail is lost or camouflaged,
brown fur on deep brown tome.

I am as lost in this floor after floor
of books, of Chinese characters
spilling from each page
into my eye, into my head
catching only the obvious Rilke,
Blake or Eliot, all

speaking now in Chinese.
Perhaps the English or the German
have been caged too long,
pacing *in cramped circles, over and over,*
seeing other tongues out there
burning brighter as the *mighty will*

of the mono-mouth *stands paralysed*.
But now you stir, yawn, and I see teeth,
their *fearful symmetry* — then
just nose and whiskers again,
and is that a grin, old and knowing?
(I smell all tongues, all mouths

as you all bend towards me,
and I understand — do you?)
But it's a challenge to plumb
your polyglot dreaming,
so I try and bend to stroke
your crown, that world of tongues,

but you bristle, snarl, and teeth again
plunging into my heart, then gone.

SQUIG

It's a squig, that sudden movement in the undergrowth.
— Ian Gentle, Illawarra artist 1945–2009

Tell me, Ian, what is a squig — this quick,
Oddly truant word wriggling from the bush
Of your beard, the glint in your eye? The flick
Of tail, perhaps like all of us, is hushed,
Awaiting the logic of its name: *squig*.
Then it quivers on the gallery wall,
Waking the cockatoo, the croc, the league
Of shadows in your heart, your hands that call
The bush to sing and shiver with delight.
Gently, gently, you coax them all alive —
Ah, what grit of sandstone, what grace of light
Perpetual as the eucalypt. This drive,

This urge to be, the squig of art, your home
Deep down, the primal wriggle in the bone.

WATER DRAGONS

Morning ablution:
face leans over
porcelain

and knuckle
hits the rim
it rings

temple bell
timeless note
then water

and the blue
dragons move
spines

arched, tongues
flickering
scales

rippling in
water warmed
with blue

fire tendrils
as if their mouths
were roots

of vines curling
from the temple
threshold

where the note
is held, held
until face

enters water, this
mundane ritual
made

strange, because
a porcelain poet
thought

to paint a washbasin
with blue, blue
dragons

AN ARGUMENT IN GLASS

For Jennifer Kemarre Martiniello,
Aboriginal glass artist

As you hold me,
you think your fingers know
I'm glass magic,
this slip and slide on cool satin,
then suddenly I'm water
and an eternity of greens —
O song of sea flowers,
you make drowning
beautiful.
Or so you say.

But what of other shades
or shadows?

From umber to gumnut brown,
we are the ancient corals
that you presume are dead.
But look: our eyes are open,
our mouths are open.
Do not forget us.
Do not resist us.
We are the dead that refuse to die
surging through
the eternal greens underwater:
emerald, seaweed, pine, juniper,
moss, crocodile, olive, lime,
chartreuse with tufts of yellow
like light flickering
and red
like blood insisting:
We are here.

Look deeply.
I'm glass magic
only when you see us.

THE COLOUR OF EYES

For Banduk Marika, Yolngu artist

After your story of the funeral, August 1991

Black, Banduk, is the colour of eyes
like night shrunk
when grandma tidies after grief.
Perhaps she could not spill
to stain the room.

Black, Banduk,
this quaver fisted
in her throat —
it has no moon,
it aches with too much swallowing.
There is no voice
to bruise the air.

You think
she wills it neat?

Tonight she smooths the black
from trembling.
She promises,
This dark will keep.

She is too frugal
when she can not weep.

*

On seeing your prints defying margins

Black that could not spill
to stain the room.

How tiny, how contained
like frugal woodblock prints
assigning loss a space.

But whose eyes
assign loss and
space — or colour?

Mine, the gallery's,
the press', the Parliament's?
No. You leap

your art, your Country
beyond the frame
beyond the page.

ODE TO A FUNERARY RELIC

Classics Museum, The Australian National University

O still marble slab
behind museum glass,
did you just stir?

A ripple in the ear —
a child's cry,
a breath snagged?
It rings, loud
as your Latin inscription —

*To the departed spirit of M. Seruilius Gemellus, who lived
9 years, 2 months and 27 days: set up by his parents
Stephanus and Fortunata for their dutiful son and
for themselves and for their [?] descendants —*

Ripples through
my own womb
that never knew a child,
and I'm pulled back to the 27th
(or was it the 28th day),
pulled into you,
back to the 1st or 2nd century AD,
your solid stillness suddenly
flesh —

hand of Stephanus
on brow of Seruilius
as he shuts eyes
arms of Fortunata
as she holds limbs
holds back departure.

O still testimony
passed on to us
descendants of loss,
always flesh
and never relic.

THE STONE MAGISTRATES

Fragment of sarcophagus
— Museo Arqueológico de Córdoba

I want to touch your faces,
your broken mouths,
your barely perceptible ears,
and feel you whisper,
feel you listen
leaning against each other
in marble bas relief,
all wide-eyed, dry-eyed
over this death.

(Whose death — and
is this a mourning?)

But it is forbidden
in museums:
my wonder could
contaminate your silence,
my flesh could
defile your stone.
Only a fragment,
only seven men
conjoined mouth to ear.

(In some secret accord
or conspiracy?)

An airless frieze:
the tight company
of bodies erect, alert

inspires a claustrophobic
dignity. And what does
the second man whisper
to the third,
him with the fist
held close to his gut?

(A death avenged or
a death arranged?)

Paleocristiano, Siglo IV:
artefact labelled thus
with a query added:
depicting magistrates?
Even experts are uncertain —
but the seventh man
clutches a tightly
rolled scroll that might
hold the truth.

(But whose truth
and for whom?)

Only a fragment
pieced with what
we think we know:
Brutus stabbed Caesar,
Pilate crucified Christ,
and through history,
lives have been judged and
taken by (our reading of) the law
certainly writ in stone.

HOW TO SPIN

PIED FANTAIL

Palago,
Ning reckons.
Tagbaya,
Father insists.
Listen,
Mother hushes
us all

trying to name you,
fix you
darting from
branch to branch,
black tail
white-rimmed

opening
closing
fan flirting
with our awe
and wish to catch
you white-throated

singer
but how nimbly
you slip
from words,
your notes deft
as your wings

beak
eyes
uncatchable
in any tongue —
Listen, mother
says again,

finger to mouth,
knowing how
no wit or will,
not even
the word itself,
can catch joy.

THE GLASSMAKERS

Canberra Glassworks

The stage is set.
Brian, Belinda, Jenni
and desire.

Spinning now
could be an orange lollipop on a stick.
No, a sunset turning and turning

then plunged into water
and retrieved as if from a bath,
a baby laid on a wooden cradle.

No, a new planet,
a blown egg veined with flowers
or a crystal ball

that cannot tell its own fortune or fate:
what it will become
in the fire womb

or in the water,
or in Brian's hands, with Belinda's breath,
or Jenni's dream.

See the little wings rising slowly
like sharp hillocks
testing the air,

its own creature now
pitting wills with
the magic makers.

Because glass is
its own desire
in its own good time and space,

suddenly a fish scaled
in seaweed, anemone and coral
all at once, tendrils of its own song,

or about to be —
is that a stingray —
no, look at its mouth,

an O
in awe
of its own becomings,

as in this
mouth to mouth,
magic makers both,

the blower and the blown
become stranger
than themselves

spinning and spun
like accidental omens:
mouth oracular

ever on the verge
of something else —
O look, the mouth

is now an eye
of a storm
not of wind and water

but wind and fire,
spinning round
suddenly a telescope

to peek through
for underwater constellations —
Andromeda, Orion, Crux

or simply
the iris of my eye,
a sunburst.

WHEN JENNI SPINS GLASS

I hear secrets
spiral into
trumpet
conch
flute,
their innards
winding
like a throat
or my cochlea.

How is it
that I hear secrets
when I touch
eel trap
dillybag
fish basket?
All in glass
but susurrations all:

rushes, sedge, sargasso, bush flowers.
Wind, loam, light, creek, soul:
what I catch
or what catches me,
the startled fish,
the wild plum,
the word
the note
the breath

still tuning in
still tuning in.

HOW TO SPIN

On tilted earth
we revolve with the flowers
balance heel to toe
with the seasons.
At each turn
here's hoping
for reverent gravity,
our roots firmer
yet friendlier
even with the stones.

*

O littlest fish
teach us how
the tiniest ripple
consumes you
head to tail
throws your life
on the line,
so we mind
even our little finger
tickling the water.

*

Dancer of mine,
I cannot love
your knees enough.
Such efficiency
unseen
unlauded.

63

Art
must not betray
its labour.
Keep
the pirouette
clean.

But those
unlovely bumps
are the miracle:
two little worlds
holding you
as you spin.

                    *

Father spins long ago
because it's all
that he remembers:
the birds whose
names have gone
extinct yet how bright
their plumage
in his memory.
(But not our names
unrecalled, unsayable.)
Then there's the boy
who looks like him,
he says, ploughing
the rice paddies
with the buffalo
that broke his arm.
Its name too
rings clear as the day

he met his sweetheart
in the green dress
but her name
is not my mother's.

*

Grandmother behind the wheel
knows how thread
comes to being:
the pinch-pull-and-slide
from heart-to-arm-
to-wrist-to-fingers-
and-then-back.
She knows
this revolution.

Now the loom,
threads interlacing
singular then multiple
disappearing in accord.
Such ease in rapport
a loosening-tightening
in the muscle
moored to the first thread
the guiding vein.
It assures her:
the margins hold the centre
the margins shape the whole.

So how she cares
for the edges
the invisible threads
their bond.
How she knows
that each must breathe
in the push-and-pull
the give-and-take
of kinship.

How I hope
we know as much
that hands and heart and will
can spin governments
that do not fray.

*

The Minister also spins
conspiracies-battles-
visions-epics
streamlined into Truth
that holds us
at the edge
of our seats 24/7
before the telly.

O Mesmer extraordinaire,
suddenly we're lifted
like Chagall's lovers
flown out of our lounge rooms

over roofs and birds
into some secret
cubicle called
the polling booth
where we tick your name
affirm your Truth.

This is no accident of composition:
how we keep you
in your Seat
ensconced and still
spinning.

*

Planetary is the will
of birds and cyclones.
Always the circular intent:
the flight from north to south and back,
whirlpool growing an eye
bent on completion
like the revolution of the earth
around the sun.

All turn
from the first urge
to go visiting
in space
only to return
where it all began
and the arc
comes full circle.

But not strangely
birds and cyclones
wear a tail,
a stray dash
in the geometry
to propel the initial lift
of will or the exit lash
at those left behind:

flowers stones
fish dancer
Father Grandmother
and the Minister
in mid-spin.

Rarely can we unspin
before all is halted.

DREAM OF OCEANS

Fernando de Magallanes had a thing
for water: the vaster and more strange,
the deeper his longing.
Perhaps he was a thirsty man,
the thirst so punishing,
he renounced Portugal in 1517
when the king did not listen,
turned his back on his boyhood
in Queen Leonora's court
and his nightly dream
of cloves, to seek new waters.

Or perhaps it was those cloves
all along, nailing him in place
to spin a tale for the Spanish King,
Charles the First, eighteen
and heady with the dream
of this Portuguese now swearing
allegiance to the Spanish crown,
this explorer, this new Castilian
promising treasures only
ever dreamt of and
All for my King.

What Sire would say no?
Kings are more thirsty,
tongues dry as throats
bellies deep wells
no ocean could fill

and ears attuned to the call of voyage
in their name — pushing His Majesty's
world beyond the flat horizon,
rounding it like the crown on his head
spinning might and right
blessed by the Church,
the birthright to rule made holy —
Dios salve el Rey.

Kings know no border
for the sacred — it is always
sovereign. So when Magallanes dreamt
of ships and men as thirsty
enough to leave mothers, fathers,
wives, sweethearts, children, friends
and the certainty of tierra
to sail westward for the first time,
His Majesty raised his sceptre
to the sky, home of Padre Nuestro
Que Estás en Los Cielos
and acquiesced,
Thy will be done.

Perhaps neither His Majesty nor Magallanes
dreamt of the curse of oceans.
After you drink them,
what remains
in the mouth, throat, gut
is salt, salt, salt
and unquenchable thirst
like fire.

FISH GOSSIP

While they are flying, the others run along back of them under the water following the shadow of the flying fish. The latter have no sooner fallen into the water than the others immediately seize and eat them. It is in fine a very amusing thing to watch.
— *Magellan's Voyage Around the Globe*, Antonio Pigafetta

> *Look, each more than three of us in length*
> *but what awkward extensions*
> *flailing about, shadowing us.*

> *And noisy as their hulk*
> *with those giant wings.*

> *But can't fly.*

The dorado rolled its eyes,
twin globes fixed on the hunt,
and the albacore bristled, fins taut,
and the bonito, blue indignant, humphed
at the men gawking from the deck
of Magellan's flagship Trinidad.

Under the puffed up sails,
Pigafetta noted:
three types of fish, each
one braza and more in length
hunting flying fish, the colondrini,
one palmo and more in length and very good to eat.

So the chronicler spins the tale
that rounds the earth.
But what's the circumference of a spin,
that revolution of an urge?
Is it not the distance between the need
to story and to feed?

No, listen, each word writ
is more than gossip
(and never quite a conversation
with fishes). I write therefore I am
while fishes eat their kind.
And never us twain shall meet.

There is no rounding
of intentions, not even
in the open sea — I tame
wind, wave, word
by the grace of God,
The Word made Flesh,

my flesh made word —
the pen slides, the lines curl.
There are flourishes in Pigafetta's
script, like flying fishes
shadowing each line, the thrust
of the tale, of the urge.

The bonito, the dorado, the albacore
are catching each, even before
they land. On the deck,
the men gawk, flail and hurl
their net, fingers crossed for some
share of the feast — because

the Captain-general and his Italian
must be the first to feed.

MUSIC: BETWEEN PIGAFETTA AND COOK

They played so harmoniously that one would believe they
possessed good musical sense. Those girls were very beautiful
and almost as white as our girls and as large.
— Pigafetta, (at the reception of the King of Cebu, 9 April 1521)

Their features were far from being disagreeable; their Voices
were soft and tunable, and they could easily repeat any
word after us.
— James Cook (at anchor, Endeavour River, 10 July 1770)

A remarkable find:
they're musical and tunable
in these backwaters.
There a naked shoulder
close to what shoulders are
at home — when we chance
on them by accident.

Listen to it move
as she raises an arm
to hit the gong — resounds
through the Captain-general,
perhaps a tiny shiver there.
Now, shoulder to breasts
tensing as she hits it again,

and again the pulse
on his cheek as if hit.
Por Dios y por todos los Santos,
they should cover up,
these beautiful heathens
as large as our girls:
a remarkable find.

Now voices, voices
like birds at dawn,
waking us up from dream
into exigency and quick resolve:
Say, bird — b-b-b-errr-d.
Say, fish — f-f-f-i-shhh.
Yes, food — f-f-f-ooo-d.

The old man with the agreeable
face stares at another Captain
(gesticulating to the sky,
the river, then his stomach),
and thinks: this white fella
is almost musical,
but pity that slight stammer.

THE STRING OF BEADS

[Magellan] gave them many knives, scissors, mirrors, bells,
and glass beads; and those two having their hands filled with
the said articles, the captain-general had two pairs of manacles
brought, such as are fastened on the feet.
— Pigafetta (On the giants of Patagonia, 1520)

The String of Beads, etc., we had left with the Children last
night were found laying in the Hutts this morning; probably
the Natives were afraid to take them away.
— Cook (At anchor, Botany Bay, 1770)

Between Magellan and Cook
is a string of beads:
bright, sparkly trinket
from their side of the world
and how exotic to the native
eye — but neither men
would dream of circling
them around the necks
of their wives:

Beatriz and Elizabeth
awaiting news at home,
wishing for the arc
to come full circle,
leavetaking and homecoming
finally knotted
like those urgent deals
with the natives: your water

for my beads,
your fish for my mirror —
see how it sparkles around
your neck (a noose
around the world,
my string of beads).
It's trade, free and fair
but sometimes we improvise
to ease the hand that gives and takes.

So beware the string of beads:
the children knew this then
and now. In an orphanage,
nine year old Dina
embroiders a collar:
30 pesos a piece to circle
the neck of a nice lady
in Sydney. How nice,
the poor dear has a job.

So beware the string of beads:
its reach is long, faraway
and endless — a knot
is tied around your neck
even before more beads
are sooner improvised.
So be vigilant:
there is something eternal
about rapacious kindness.

BETWEEN BEATRIZ AND ELIZABETH

Magellan had fallen in April, 1521; in September
of that same year his little son Rodrigo dies, and by
March, 1522 Magellan's wife Beatriz had learned
from the Portuguese Indies of the fate of her husband.
— *Historic Ships*, Rupert S. Holland

[Elizabeth] also kept a small, coffin-shaped, wooden
'ditty box' which held a tiny painting of Cook's death
and a lock of his hair.
— Australian National Maritime Museum

He turns: first arc
of a ship towards
the full circle of

the world
the Antarctic.

He turns: last arc
of a shoulder away
from the door and

Beatriz
Elizabeth.

She turns and turns,
circumnavigates grief
a hundred times over.

Her arc: only a footnote
in history.

GIRL ON THE LAMP

From Romana Córdoba, Siglo l
— Museo Arqueológico de Córdoba

Who are you
that looks back at us,
lights us
saves us
from the dark,
knows us
each night
more than we'll ever
know ourselves?

(At 11, 17, or 27,
knowing more or less.)

But on closer
look, it could be
your eyes are closed,
dreaming
raring
to be saved
from the dark yet
spinning into it
so knowing even more.

(Our deep hopes,
our long longings.)

Is it the witching hour
in ancient Rome or Córdoba,
and have the girls let out
their hair
bristling
like yours etched
on bronze and
chins up
with your resolve?

(Knowing Veturia married at 11,
bore 6 babies, died at 27.)

Artefact of girlhood
arrested, is this
your story too?
And did you light
her tears,
her blood
on the wedding night,
the births, then the vigil
for the dead?

(Hoping to sit by the fire,
longing to see Mother again.)

To be saved
or not to be saved
from the dark:
this is the question.
But even salvation
is in the hands
of men —
what do they know
of our dark?

(Bloodstain on the sheets even
before the monthly blood began.)

Girl on the lamp
from antiquity,
we think ourselves safe
in the 21st Century
when we spin,
light our own
darknesses,
salvations,
or so we think.

(Mother said, trust only
the fire from our hearth.)

Girl on the lamp,
there is a hole
under your chin,
for the wick?
And another, for the oil?
Lit, perhaps your hair
bristled more
like the Gorgon's,
awake and wide-eyed.

(Mother said, now stare —
stare down that man into stone.)

DRAGON BRIDE

Late afternoon against the mountains
and the dark river: in their white lace,
beads and tulle, three brides. The grooms
are there too, dancing attendance like
the wedding artists and their cameras.

There is a threat of rain, a slight fog.
The mountains are grey and the brides
are serious, solemn. One is in the water
to her thighs, veil floating among her
pink carnations. I think Ophelia, but

perhaps the eye of the lens sees
water nymph in the dreamy undulations
of tulle and river. Back to us, she rests
her chin on the crook of her shoulder,
and looks back, in an afterthought,

to her groom on the bank. No smile.
Perhaps it is this river: Yulong —
meeting the dragon that sets the tone.
Further up, the other bride at least
holds the hand of her groom: a couple.

But it is the third bride that arrests us.
Hers is off-white, as if soaked in subtle
tea and like skin on her: arc after arc
of her in arc after arc of lace scallops
descending to her feet into a train

stretching nearly the length of a raft
where she stands, bareheaded, still,
arms outstretched to the mountains,
clutching the yards of her tulle veil
trailing behind her, gossamer mist

in the wind. The pose is defiant, almost
imperious, as if calling out to the arcs
and arcs of grey in the distance, sisters
to her form, incantatory in this dusk
that wonders: who is she marrying?

Tonight, her groom will be oblivious.
In the bridal chamber, she will turn
and her lace will shimmer into scales,
her train will flick into a tail, and he
will taste salt: it is he who will bleed.

CROW TURNING

Pagputi ng uwak — when the crow turns white,
his fist will turn into palm, tender on my cheek.

Where the crow flies backward, the clouds
will return, then the rain, tender on my cheek.

On the dry expanse further than their reach,
two women wait for any car, any tenderness.

Gloria: hopeful bride from the Philippines, two years ago.
Betty: her neighbour from the next cattle station.

Their car stalled, so they wait for any rumble
out there, wait for the red dust to stir, wait.

They hold hands, squint at the infinite blue broken only
by a crow crying, inconsolable in this two-year drought.

But with Betty here now, Gloria is as dry-eyed
as the land. They chuckle: let that crow do the crying.

They watch crow, hear crow, think crow talk:
When the crow turns white. Where the crow flies backward.

Above it turns, lands, listens: they're talking about me.
So it waits too, for any epiphany about itself.

When the crow turns white, then it will happen.
How we say it back home. When it will never happen.

(Like tenderness, like rain, like being safe. They've done this
too many times: the urgent call, the rescue, the long drive.)

Where crows fly backward is where it's remote, strange —
too strange and — very, very hard for you, I know.

The swollen lips break into a smile, radiant through the bruises.
But sometimes it is enough that someone knows.

Two women and a crow on the vast red: they all know.

TURNING A CORNER

Afternoon walk, Canberra

Watson Street
awash with 5 pm
light, sky still blue
trees still bright
but hinting shadows,
autumn oaks and eucalypts passing
from day and soon to night,

then I turn a corner

into McKay —
light stuns me,
stops me: up there illumined,
the cross, the minaret
then the dome, blue-glass windowed
against a naked oak
against unstinting blue.

A hush within
is lit — follows its kin,
light ebbing upwards
from the dome,
quickly half in shadow,

but I turn the corner

eyes now taking on
the prettiest white church
(embarrassed at the thought,
pedestrian, unholy).

On the white walls,
mosaic saints meet my gaze:
solemn, timeless,
demanding quiet.

St. Nicholas Ukrainian Orthodox Church: 1988.

A double-take —
my father, Nicolas
named after San Nicolas de Tolentino
who's named after *this* St. Nicholas of Myra?

And there's the church
of my childhood summers
in Grandmother's village of Estancia,
San Nicolas de Tolentino Parish.

I'm turning corners and corners
of disparate yet bonded histories,
walking a bit further,
drawn by a stone memorial
at the gate —

Execution by Hunger
1932–1933

... a man-made famine claimed the lives of
more than 7,000,000 men, women and children
in Ukraine. This enforced famine-genocide was
perpetrated by the regime of the Communist Party
of the U.S.S.R. as a consequence of the resistance
of the Ukrainian nation to Russian occupation ...

My breath catches,
light within extinguished.
No more corners
to turn — stay with me, witness me,
demands the inscription.

I meet the eyes
of St. Nicholas: look
and look closer,
they say.

I stay for a long while.

On my way home,
I turn the same corner
and look back: the cross, the minaret
the dome all in shadow — it's 6 pm.

On Watson now,
shadowy Watson taking my feet
towards other hungers,
other executions ongoing,

towards a passage
through kindred histories.
We've known the path so well,
yet never quite learned

how to turn a corner.

WHEN GLOBE TURNS VERB

It spins faster
than how she urges it,
China sliding past against her palm,
then Morocco then America then —

Daddy, where's Busay?
Cheryl is six and keen,
perched on her father's desk
turning and turning

the antique globe
passed on from his own father
by his father's father
who built ships

shrinking the globe
even more as shares
were floated from continent
to continent, rounding

dream then empire
spinning now under
a tiny palm. *Daddy,*
it isn't here.

What isn't what,
sweetheart?
Teresa said she lived
under a tall, tall

volcano in Busay,
but it isn't here!
The globe spins faster.
Always it's the right

pressure of the palm
that turns it: now a thing,
a noun — then moving,
more verb than noun.

Teresa who, sweetie?
Oh, Daddy, Mummy's new
maid Teresa — her house
went whoosh, she said,

under hot mud and
burning rocks — whoosh
and gone, Daddy!
Gone where, Cheryl?

The globe slows down
to a halt. *Busay, Daddy,*
Teresa's home —
it's not on your globe.

Daddy finally looks up
from the awaited tweet
from China: *Deal sealed.*
He lifts his daughter

from his desk,
spins her around
in his Manhattan study.
How about a gelato,

sweetheart, to celebrate?
She squeals in delight
at each turn
of her doting father,

and on his desk,
it watches, knowing:
when globe turns globalised,
some can celebrate.

PHOENIX COOKS BREAKFAST

For Chunfeng

Every night, drumming for an hour, a rhythm
Singular and resolute as purpose, because daily

Phoenix must rise before the morning mist rises
From the mountains to cook breakfast for the poets

Unaware it's the rhythm of her chopping each night
That orchestrates with their keyboard tapping

So in the morning they can feast on East and West:
From stir-fried noodles to bacon and eggs,

Even passionfruit seeded and juiced till late last night
And chopsticks and cutlery, whichever is their pleasure

And the mountains look on at Phoenix pleasing,
Her nightly drumming, her quiet coming and going

With no English, thus unheard, unseen by the poets
With no Chinese, but Phoenix rises to any need or wish

Missed, any pleasure gap, and the mountains look on
Bonded to her silence, knowing how it is to endlessly

Look and be looked at by poets awed on a full stomach,
Then at 3 pm when the kitchen rituals are done,

Phoenix sits under the laundry hanging on the top floor,
Looks back at the mountains, and if the poets look,

They may witness a conversation between those
Who know how hard it is to please in silence.

But on their final breakfast before departure,
The poets wish to have their photo taken

With Phoenix and the mountains, but she cannot
Rise to the occasion, her hands and feet cold:

She has never had her picture taken before,
Was never looked at, was never made an image

To feed the pleasure of a poet.

IMAGINE LENNON IN YANGSHUO

No heaven, no hell, no religion, no country,
and so a world in one accord.

Let's imagine these and more, John,
when bombs take children in Syria,
Palestine, Iraq, Afghanistan, Pakistan
and every other place you or I
have never visited but imagine,
every country, city, town, village,
home visited by the bullet,
every child's heart arrested,
every child's name fed to the earth,
then let's write the longest poem with nothing
but names — a poem that will never
finish, even if the end
is known: wars never finish.

But we are at peace with the dragon
river, John (forgive the intimate
address), among the karst mountains
in a restaurant hotel where the menu
is in English and they're playing you
again like you'll never finish,
and my vegetable soup is hot-herby
(they added ginger and garlic
for my cold) — here you only
have to ask, and imagine they will,
readily, and serve it to you
with a smile, you don't even
have to tip — the yuan knows

No heaven, no hell, no religion, no country,
and so a world in one accord.

You're not the only dreamer,
nor am I — and *xie xie* we say
to all who help us dream,
write gold records, Grammy wonders
or just little poems — help us sit
in a restaurant hotel where the menu
is in English and they're playing you
again like you'll never finish,
and my vegetable soup is hot-herby —
help us from hot stove, sink, counter
of infinite labour for our need
is never finished, ever
demanding a smile that knows

No heaven, no hell, no religion, no country,
and so a world in one accord.

Let's imagine their own dreams, John
(forgive me again for the intimate
address, polite formality is Golden
Rule here): to travel to your country,
sit in a restaurant hotel where the menu
is in Chinese, and the Liverpudlian
chef says yes to any added ginger,
garlic, chilli, if at hand, to make
them feel at home with all of us
no doubt now truly globalised
so we do unto others what others do
unto us at either side of the world
still turning despite Brexit, imagining

No heaven, no hell, no religion, no country,
and so a world in one accord.

A BOY NAMED DENMARK

Against whirlwinds, he looks sixteen
but perhaps he's mid-twenties.
Here, Ma'am, he offers me a bowl
of blueberries and pomegranate seeds,
his smile bright as his nameplate
announcing — a country?

On white porcelain, blood-red
they glow, a bed of rubies
for the blueberries, sweet perfect
as this hour. Against whirlwinds,
he shines even brighter when I say,
Salamat — Thank you.

Denmark is as Filipino as I am.
And he has a brother named Merlin?
Magic. It must be Camelot
at the Emirates business lounge,
a hush impeccable and cool
in the middle of the desert.

The champagne is Moët,
the salads fresh from some oasis
garden, the cuisine 5-star East & West,
the chocolates designer brands,
and all around, the Philippine
topnotch service reigns supreme.

Sorry, Ma'am, with us here,
there's – incoming word weighed —
discrimination. Incoming too, a storm,
my sense of justice: I think of race, class
and how within these whirlwinds,
the Filipino waiters come and go.

It's wallpaper, comes with the job
like the smile required of servitude.
I'll take care of you, Ma'am —
but the others take care only of those
who might tip — pangkain, Ma'am.
Suddenly the arc rounds: I get it.

They discriminate the travellers.
Who might tip, who might not.
Pangkain: tips for daily meals
so wages can go home.
And it's Verlin, my brother,
I'm sending him to university.

He glows with pride, now a head
taller against the whirlwinds
of the wallpaper behind him,
perhaps inspired by back home.
Our kosikos weave, squares with
arcs rippling, turning square

spherical and eternally spinning.
Kosikos: whirlwind. It's a trick
in the eyes, a clever feat —
imagine how far our art has come
all the way to this wall, like you and I.
Magic, Denmark. We speak more

in our language, and rubies
crunch in my mouth, how sweet
the blood-leap of kinship
as we bask in our resolved circle,
his words and mine, each an arc
conjoining in the sounds of home

and the squares of our distant lives
suddenly made spherical. Magic.
Can I get you anything else, Ma'am?
Imagine that, Ma'am, we're from
the same city too, even if you're
Australian now. I thrall over

the eternal movement, begin
to write this poem, awaiting
Denmark with my ordered water
as behind *The New York Times,*
my partner stirs: *This research*
on human origins is fascinating.

We all come from Africa,
it's in the DNA, but in different waves.
The wall rises, waves rippling
as a ruby splinter catches
in my tooth. An irritation
I push out with my tongue.

Denmark returns with my water.
I show him my author's website,
my list of books — *Please give me*
the link, Ma'am — I do and
$20 in tip — flustered, he takes
my hand, touches it to his brow

as we do back home, in reverence
of our elders. Open, my hand holds
magic in place (I'm moved-I'm kind)
and the arc ripples in my wrist
but the ruby splinter nags,
still in my tooth, as he cleans up.

I'll read them all, Ma'am,
your books, so I can get inspired
and maybe be like you.
The ruby digs in, deep,
again pomegranate, real
and the squares return, angles sharp

as the optic trick slaps me on the face:
I'm only in transit briefly before
a Spanish holiday. Denmark transits
forever with his tray, his route between
the bar and a traveller's desire serviced
with her own version of magic.

PLEASE FORWARD

After the watchtowers of Jiangmen

It must have passed many hands
from New Gold Mountain,
must have lost its crisp white
and the depth of the red band
running a path at its centre,
must have had its ink smudged
by sweat or damp as it passed
more mountains, crossed ocean
and rivers to get to Dawan,

yet the flourish of a father's
hand is indelible: *This letter*
contains eight pounds in total.
Please forward it to my son …
It is 1851 in Melbourne, perhaps
a cold winter in the mines and
the fingers are numb but swift
with the brush as a year's labour
is folded, tucked under a shirt

just above the heart — *please*
forward, he hears his own
calligraphy, as if each stroke
were now this path home
and his heartbeats, quick steps
chasing the course of the ink
as he turns off the lamp and
lies on his mat. Tomorrow,
he will hand it over: *Please*

forward — but he can't sleep.
Character after character spins
off the paper, chasing shadows
from the crisp white and the red
band that makes him think
of blood — in Dawan, bandits
are marauding; in Melbourne,
his New Gold Mountain,
the ground is cold and hard

on his back — will his son reach
the only watchtower in time?
Please forward, he hears
the plea of his own hand,
even as each character finds
its way back to the paper
safe, indelibly forwarded
across centuries. Here it is,
an envelope in museum glass.

It has passed many hands,
has lost its crisp white and
the depth of the red band
running a path at its centre,
has had its ink smudged,
yet it stands, a watchtower
to ward off the bandits of time
that may steal the memory
of a father writing to his son.

Please forward this remembering.

WELLSPRING IN ALFACAR

An archaeological excavation chanced upon by accident
— 1 October 2016, Alfacar (where Lorca was shot?)

The Physics professor takes my hand
and we descend into the earth,
ochres and shadows grainy
with histories known yet unknown.
The sun descended way ahead,
as had the others never met

but maybe here, here: aqui

in my ear, their possibility
whispered by the linguist — esperanza
translated into hope urging on
the archaeologist, voice clear as air
but no comprendo his science in Spanish,
so the linguist perseveres as we descend.

Hear, hear the layers of tierra:

first, imposed earth, reddish
diggings for a soccer field,
then *natural earth*, a little darker,
and deeper down a new stratum
almost white surprisingly — I think of bones,
then the main hole, darkest brown

large enough to curl up in

for the night — but I'm a stranger here,
so tread softly, tenderly and
listen with equal tenderness
(as a mother does to her singing child)
to this translated possibility: this could be it,
the well. The referents are here.

Hypothesis, or wish, or longing:

Let them be here. Presumptuous,
I've descended into the archaeologist's
heart, as I translate his excavation.
My language fills his hole,
singing over his science
(or a mother's singing child).

What is the tune of longing?

But I'm a stranger here,
the professor, the linguist, the archaeologist
understand — and wish for me to understand.
So they translate, translate,
but the shadows are fully descended now,
I can't see their faces.

It is their breaths I understand.

Comprendo: breaths, little notes
against my skin, into my ear
circling the square hole, softening angles,
arcs of air connecting arcs of histories
of griefs known and unknown —
perhaps how a mother sings

back to her singing child:

Silencio ahora, querido, y escucha.
So the square becomes a sphere,
a whole note spun into ovum of the earth
fitting us all in: Fernando the professor,
Encarni the linguist, Javier the archaeologist,
and Merlinda, Magdalena, Reinis,

all listeners now — and all named

unlike the others we have yet to meet
if they are here, here: aqui
in this well, this wellspring of histories
of the desaparecidos from a war as long ago
as a longing, perhaps soon to be found:
hear them breathe again

into our ears, our lungs,

so we can find how the living and the dead
come full circle, all tender now
with each other, with those just met,
might never meet — I wonder how
one finally meets face to face
with a longing, so I ask

the archaeologist about his heart:

How does your corazon cope
with this job? So he tells the story
of how once he unearthed a skull
while a sister waited above ground,
hoping, hoping *this*
is *mi hermana*.

From his eyes, water wells,

his heart excavated out
in the open. But he could only offer
his science: the long awaited skull
was not her sister, and yet, and yet
she begged: *Let me, please,*
embrace it anyway –

suddenly we're all embraced

aqui, aqui en el corazon
of a sister brother father mother
singing back to a beloved singing back
the breath of the living to the dead
welling up from the deep
and singing back, singing back:

Silencio ahora, queridos, y escuchan, escuchan.

2006. At Bar Aixa in Granada, the bartender shrinks,
face growing dark when I ask about La Pena Negra —
No, no, no, he waves his hand to ward me off.
Then at the Moroccan café of As-Sirat, Leila tells me
it means *the black pity* and it can swallow you.

It's the feared sombra, the shadow: flamenco's mark
coursing through Lorca, his duende's cry wrenched
from the throat between laughter and mourning and
exaltation, but always negra, a dark where we can't
even see our own hand held close to our face.

But then, in Córdoba your hand flicks a red mantilla,
carves the air again and again like a bleeding scimitar
as you turn, turn and the duende plays hide and seek
in the arc of roja, roja, its heartbeat the click and stamp
of your feet, imperious, joyous, lethal all at once.

2016. You, flamenco dancer, invoke the bullring as we cry
Ole, O Dios! Smiling, you dance La Pena Roja, not of
the death of the bull or matador, but of the darker residue
of red in our eyes, of blood drawn in sport, in combat,
in the pugilism growing darker still in our veins.

Ole, how stained we are! We dance: arc after arc of red,
of blood, of death, and smile, triumphantly smile.

THE STORY OF BLUE

Brought to China from Iran, cobalt was called Huiqing, Muslim Blue.
— East Asia: A New History, Hugh Dyson Walker

She circumnavigates the rim of the cup with a finger:
once for worry, twice for deep thought. Now it's six
times underwater in the sink, but pausing on a chip only
her seasoned finger knows. A world wounded six times

over, she sighs, tracing the Chinese pagoda still as blue
as the willow swaying in that breeze she swears she feels
when she sips her tea. It's the only cup left of great
grandmother's Willow Pattern set sent home to London

two decades after the family's stint with the East India
Company. Too much breaking through the years. But always,
there was tea: through the Opium Wars, 5 cups out of 6,
the Indian Rebellion, 4 cups, then the First World War

in England, 2 later wrapped in grandmother's wedding
dress sailed all the way to Sydney. White and blue, as blue
as the sky, her mother used to tell her. A blue to die for,
as her brother did on the Kokoda track. Again she hears

how it shattered at her mother's feet when the letter came,
so this orphan cup. Again she pauses on the chip that only
her finger knows. Only a tiny ping it was. Cup against
the tap after her guest had left. After he had asked,

Whose blue, whose sky, whose orphanhood? How dare he
shatter their history? 5 cups, then 4, then 2, then 1. But only
a tiny ping of anger it was at this sink. One can't be precious
about breakage these days. TV news is infested with it

and the shards we sweep under the carpet to survive.
But she remembers the blue bit that cut her hand when
she helped her mother clean up after. Bit of that willow
swaying in the breeze, as if it were a balmy spring day.

She'd never seen so much red on the white tea towel.
So how dare he ask her what about the other colours,
this son of hers come home from another war in the East,
eyes bloodshot and speaking in tongues: *That blue is not*

English or Chinese, mum, it's Muslim Blue, don't you know that?
And the story is not always about us. She circumnavigates
the rim of the cup with a finger, the sixth spin longing
to round her world wounded by the wound of her own blood.

AT LA MEZQUITA

I belong to the beloved, have seen the two
worlds as one and that one call to and know,

first, last, outer, inner, only that
breath breathing human being.
— *Only Breath*, Jelaluddin Rumi. Trans. Coleman Barks

Over and over, the arc, and so we spin half a world,
half a wish — now awed, now arrested at 180 degrees
of the arco de herradura, the horseshoe or keyhole arch
becoming double becoming manifold, like light
streaming from wherever and whenever, so hard to know
how to turn, like a pretend sufi bewildered at the door.

This is our becoming, over and over, that we peek into,
slip into, and neither is the key quite fully turned.
For we are breakers and broken through histories
as manifold in their own arcs, own ways of turning.
Do we fall on our knees, pray, chant, raise our palms
to push each arc higher, deeper, so we can squeeze through

to enter a mosque, a cathedral, or earlier yet, a Phoenician
or Roman doorway? Does it matter now? In the garden outside
the oranges are fully turned before they've even ripened,
all 360 degrees in knowing each belongs to each beloved
hand, *Not Christian or Jew or Muslim, not Hindu, Buddhist,*
sufi, or zen, but *only that breath breathing human being.*

ARC OF ARCS

I am in awe
of quarter turns
presaging revolution.

Toes pivot east
towards the roses.

> *Bloomed, yes,*
> *as she laboured,*
> *announcing me —*
> *Mamá grew them too*
> *in Manila*, her mother said.
> So in Perth, Elena turns
> eastward, stretching toes, ankles,
> thighs before a run.

And heel digs its dream
of wells.

> Calcaneus, heel bone,
> stubborn to the max.
> Digs in, twists,
> burrows on red earth —
> *This is my Country,*
> *wells deep with water*
> *not steam,*
> *so frack off!*

And waist swivels
against a palm.

O the arc of it,
that silk, that moist
moment, that almost love
in the dance hall —
kept safe, deep
in his gunner's palm
taut and ready,
C'mon, take a swing!

And neck snaps
to the right.

Yet the twinge
is in her left shoulder,
ripples down her back
as she ducks in time
the fist, the whitest knuckle
aimed at her jaw as she breathes
to the top of her lungs,
You f—cking bastard!

And wrist wakes
to an intent,

the axis,
friend to the arc,
even before it's born
or reborn — from fist
to palm: *Here Miriam,
here Ahmed, here Samya,
here fish, here bird,
here my hand, take it.*

109

So I am in awe
of quarter turns, or even less.
The toes, heel, waist,
neck, wrist know them
before we know them.
Herald to the full circle,
O that arc of arcs

towards the roses,
        homage to Gran who grew them too,
towards redreaming wells
        to how we used to dream them,
towards the girl
        who brings him home from a war,
towards free air to breathe
        us safe and free,
towards the stranger
        turning us even stranger
to who we think we are, sometimes:
fixed, riveted, unmoving,
        unmoved.

PASSAGE

IN MEDIAS RES

A swarm
You said

CrossingtheborderCrossingtheborderCrossingtheborder

Look again

Aamir Fadwa Anas Bana Rima Nisreen Ahmed
Hussein Amr Noor Ammar Lulwa Saad Fahad Ayah
Abdul Fadi Zeinah Majd Hayah Shafiqah Alyaa'
Khalid Baraa Aziza Fahmi Hassan Nahla Raqi
Ghamza Rima Zayid Tarek Rafia Aylan Yaman Raja
Danya Reem Liliane Baraka Nizar Asi Ibrahim
Sameetha Hayat Zahi Khalil Dama'a Layla Tamadur
Nasri Sami Najeeba Abdel Iman Najlaa Mahmoud
Hanan Joma'a Fouzi Qais A'ahd Badr Isar Mohammad
Fadah Sherifa Asped Adnan Kareem Kareemi Jameela

Crossing

YouYouYouYouYouYouYouYouYouYouYouYouYouYouYouYouYou

IN OUR ARMS

It is a composition:
our arms holding
a boy retrieved
from the Mediterranean.

And we pass him
around, from arm to arm
around the world,
from story to story

woven, rewoven, interwoven
with threads
of ourselves: so it is ours
now, the weight

of a three-year old body
or its absence.
And so heroic

in our grief,
we rush to write
the latest news

or blog
or song
or poem.

DOUBLE-CROSSED

We almost
met — me
with my son,
you with yours.
Both crying:
mine with hunger,
yours with loss
but the tears
fell on
the same
earth.

But no
moisture
or even flood
could soak
it through.
Our grief
just fizzled
in the heat.
Besides,
there are no
more seeds
to water.

Your life
like mine
is the driest
country

but we don't
know because
there's a wall
so high
between us,
we are both
invisible.

Only
the border guard
saw us both,
two women under
the shadow
of the wall
to-ing and fro-ing:
after our village
was sieged,
after your husband's
car was bombed.

*To keep
us safe and free,*
they said.

At the border,
we almost met
and caught
each other's eye
and saw in there
how safe we are,
how free.

GRANDMOTHER AND THE BORDER

Estancia, Philippines

Kindly listen and listen kindly.
This would have been grandmother's
advice when the neighbour, in the quiet
of the night, moved his fence closer
to our jackfruit tree, expanding his yard,
cramping our own. So the fight began
under a fruit perfuming both yards
from the jute sack that kept away the birds.
We could smell heaven all the way to both
houses, so surely it was harvest time —
but then the fence, and then the fight.

Kindly listen and listen kindly:
This, *my land's border. No, this* my
land's border. But you moved it last
night. No, you moved it a year ago and
I'm just righting the mark now, see.
I see, but whose mark, yours or mine?
But what is yours, and what is mine?
A bird circled, roosted, waited on the fence,
its beady eyes following each arc of fist
and angry voice, O that act of spleen.
Birds know things, know how to listen.

Kindly listen and listen kindly.
But Grandmother would not have been
heard, so she would have called out
to the other grandmother across the fence:

Come, give me your sharpest knife,
and both their sons would have stopped,
stepped back, like the bird hopping
further away, its little heart not quite
ready for this. Will blood be drawn?
But knife in hand, grandmother would have
harvested the jackfruit, and cut it in two.

Kindly listen and listen kindly,
she would have told anyone who listened.
This tree has stood here above our sons,
our grandchildren growing up, sitting
on this fence and looking out to both
our houses. Its fruit here knows no
fence, so here, have half of it, and
we'll have the other — but wait,
she plunged a hand into her half
and took out one yellow heart,
then fed it to the waiting bird.

So kindly listen and listen kindly,
even if now, the wise grandmothers
have passed, and the fences have
grown higher, have plunged deeper
between our houses, our voices angrier,
and the knives have come out
sharper, and it's no longer enough
that only the white blood of a tree
is drawn, staining our hands as we
feast on perfumed fruit, heart by
yellow heart, together with a bird.

EACH OTHER'S ARC

Once upon a time conjured
in Bikol, Filipino and English.
We tell it over and over again.

Digde ini nagpopoon. Anum na taon ako, siguro lima.
Si Lola nag-iistorya manongod sa parahabon nin kasag
Na nagtatago sa irarom kan kama.

Dito ito nagsisimula. Anim na taon ako, siguro lima.
Si Lola nagkukuwento tungkol sa magnanakaw ng alimango
na nagtatago sa ilalim ng kama.

This is where it begins. I am six years old, perhaps five.
Grandmother is storytelling about the crab-stealer
hiding under the bed. Each story-word crackles
under the ghost's teeth, infernal under my skin. I shiver.

But perhaps this is where it begins.
Grandfather teasing me with that lady in the hills
walking into his dream, each time a different
colour of dress, a different attitude under my skin.
I am bereft of constancy, literal
at six years old, perhaps five.

Or, this is where it begins.
Mother reviewing for her college Spanish exam:
Ojos.
Labios.
Manos.
Suddenly also under my skin, long before I understood
Eyes: how they conjure ghosts under the bed,
Lips: how they make ghosts speak,
Hands: how they cannot be silent.

119

I remember too Father gesturing, invoking
once upon a time. This is where it begins:
story, word, gesture under my skin.
At six years old, perhaps five.

And so this poem is for my father, mother,
grandmother, grandfather and all the storytellers,
the conjurers who came before us. They made us shiver
not just over crab-stealers hiding under the bed
or a lady uncertain of her garb. They made us shiver
also over faith, over tenderness.
Or that little tickle when a word hits a hidden
crevice in the ear. Just air
heralding the world or worlds we think
we dream up alone.

No, storytelling is not lonely,
not as we claim in our little rooms lit only
by a lamp or a late computer glow.
Between the hand and the pen, or the eye and the screen,
they have never left, they who storytold before us,
they who are under our skin.

Perhaps they even conjured us, but not alone.
Storytelling, all our eyes collect into singular seeing,
our lips test one note over and over again,
our hands follow each other's arc, each sweep of resolve.
Eyes, lips, hands conjoined: the umbilical cord restored.

BALLAD OF THE TURTLE AND THE GHOST

After the shooting

And so in this town they say the queen
of sea turtles swallowed the bullet.
An accident or a trail of mishaps, who knows,
but I do. I am the Pacific, the amniotic
in her, around her as she swims back
to where she was born to birth another.

Who fired it? the children asked,
and the mothers and fathers hid their faces,
not knowing what to say. But the oldest
grandmother in the village said,
*It was for a young man who turned bad
like the mango tree that never knew woodsmoke.*

(You were too busy living to make the daily fire
under its leaves and coax the goodness out.)

And so in this town, they say the queen
of sea turtles swallowed the bullet,
only one of them snagged in a plastic bag
she mistook for jellyfish while foraging
en route to nest at the base of the earth
awaiting her after a long, long swim in me.

How did it get there? the children asked.
The mothers and fathers hid their fear,
their shame. But the oldest grandmother
said, *He was hungry, buying lunch
from that stall on the beach — a plastic bag
of rice and fish, and that was that.*

(You were too busy living with your hunger,
you could not see how it got there.)

And so in this town, they say the queen
of sea turtles swallowed the bullet,
her long voyage stranded by a catch
in her throat. So, heavy with eggs,
she waited until a hungry ghost came
to the shore and began to weep.

And what happened? the children asked.
The mothers and fathers turned away,
afraid of what they'll see and know.
But the oldest grandmother said,
He begged the queen to take him with her,
because even his ghost is unwelcome here.

(You were too busy living to hear the weeping
and see me rise higher, saltier with tears.)

And so in this town they say they saw
one moonless night a ghost riding a turtle
and calling out, *O mother of mine,*
birth me a second time at the base of the earth
where I will grow flippers and a shell
hard enough to bear the curse of the unforgiven.

PIGAFETTA WEEPS

*When we wounded any of those people with our crossbow shafts, which
passed completely through their loins from one side to the other, they,
looking at it, pulled on the shaft now on this and now on that side,
and then drew it out, with great astonishment, and so died; others
who were wounded in the breast did the same, which moved us to
great compassion. [...] We saw some women in their boats who were
crying out and tearing their hair, for love, I believe, of their dead.*
— Pigafetta (in the Marianas)

It was the Islas de los Ladrones,
after all — so how the lump
in your throat
like when you ate the leather
of the ship's mainyard
with no water
to wash it down?

Ladrones: thieves.
Magellan named them
because they *entered the ships and stole*
whatever they could lay
their hands on.
Were you astonished
at such brazen act,

your lot with the civilising
quill, cross, sword
that took islands, countries
cultures, peoples?
For love, I believe,
of His Majesty.
Were you astonished

at how moved you were
at such astonishment
in dying? Pigafetta, my hand
reaches out all the way
to 1521, so I can touch
your throat, your breast
as you watched

the keening widows,
their men wrenching out
shaft after shaft
of crossbows. I wish
to wrench you here
and now, to newer keenings
and astonishments.

Like one travel writer's
on board a helicopter
touring a war zone
and I kept wondering,
is he being ironic
in his marvel
so astonishingly arresting,

line by eloquent line?
For love, for love,
we believe,
of the word, the story,
the page alive with
our little astonishing creatures
crawling towards posterity.

DREAM OF EMPIRE

And then the shore
for Ferdinand Magellan
after Mar Pacifico
that clung to his mouth,
salt so salty, it gave him visions
that returned him to his old bed
at twelve years old,
again a Portuguese
dreaming of cloves and
an ear-bird an aromatic ear
an earlobe delicate,
curve of a tear
of his wife Beatriz.
And just as salty.

But then the shore:
1521 and these dark folks
half naked yet studded
with gold. So Magellan planted
the cross guarded by the sword
to claim this land
for the King of Spain.
Still, no pageantry could vanish the salt
at the roof of his mouth
and the thirst, thirst, thirst —
but what if we seed
this shore with the sacred?

So Rajah Humabon and his Queen Humamai
were baptised. Perhaps it was a pact
devised by this knowing King of Cebu:
I take your god only
if you take on my rival
in the nearby island of Mactan,
Datu Lapu-Lapu
(that namesake of a fish).
And so to battle —
but blood is as salty,
and Magellan only tasted more of it:
his own salt now, brimming red
from his mouth at the feet
of the warrior Datu.

Salt, salt, salt seeping
from flesh to tierra to mar,
circumnavigating back the globe
to crack the gut
of the next sovereign, Felipe,
thirstier in his dreams
of those faraway islands.
So Villalobos was sent
to complete the mission,
and the archipelago of more than
7000 islands was named
after His Majesty: Las Islas Filipinas.

But no staving that thirst,
so a new voyage
from another jewel
of the imperial crown
of the new world: Mexico
from where Miguel López de Legazpi,
conquistador from soul
to sole of his boots,
sailed with the official stamp
of dominion over the Philippines
for more than 350 years
ferrying galleons of treasures:
gold, gold, gold
and more to España.

But Magellan is long gone
and the dead cannot tell
how pernicious this thirst
and how dreams are not sweet
but salty with blood, tears
and a hint of clove
that make him turn, turn, turn
in his grave — rattling skeleton
dreaming of an ear to whisper to
the story of this thirst:
infectious like the common cold,
malignant like cancer.

(And what terror for all
tasked to quench it
with new blood, new tears.)
Then Britain caught it from Spain
caught it from Portugal
caught it from France
caught it from Russia
caught it from Rome
caught it from the Ottoman
caught it from the Han
caught if from the Mongol
and so on, though who caught it
from whom is vexed,
because *Mine came first!*

But beware the contagion:
2017, and it has metastasised
into The Corporate Kingdom
armed with The Market
and gold is yellow or black
from the gut of the earth
howling war, war, war,
or blue — but not salty
water quenching thirst,
greening fields, raising animals
for meat — blue gold
fought over to the death.

Magellan turns again and again,
his skull near exploding
with the story of this thirst,
how it all began with dreams
and that ear pierced
with clove: clavus: nail.
He wants to whisper to it,
Listen, the ghost of Lapu–Lapu hovers,
exacting justice and making sovereign
new thirsts, new terrors,
or so we think. A hand longs
to lift itself from the sod
to pluck off that nail
to free that ear into listening.

But he's nothing but bone
petrified by history.
Still, the story rages in his skull.
What are new thirsts
but ancient ones,
their tears, blood, terrors
umbilical — bound
to those we sowed
in that first dream?
He struggles to lift a finger
from the sod, to point back to that first,
that even older ghost.

And when we cry murder
against the mass
surging through our borders,
do not forget how once we declared
there are no borders for the sovereign,
no borders for our right to rule
from Our Father Who Art In Heaven.
But the skull without lips,
without throat cannot whisper now,
cannot speak — it shatters
with the weight
of the forgotten tale.

Perhaps somewhere in a camp,
a refuge in a far continent,
a little girl will discover shards
like salty chalk,
and on the ground, she will begin
to write with them. It's early days,
so she will begin with
her mother's alphabet.
Perhaps years from now,
it will grow into the full story
of the thirst,
the original dream.

Perhaps we will finally listen.

PIGAFETTA'S WONDER

Pieces of gold, of the size of walnuts and eggs are found
by sifting the earth in the island of that king who came to
our ships. All the dishes of that king are gold and also some
portion of his house, as we were told by that king himself.
— Pigafetta (in Samar)

Once upon a time there was a tree
and a bird: the Piedras Platas, tree
of silver stones, home to the Adarna bird,
its tail the length of all your dreams,
Pigafetta, and all its colours:

> pearl of teeth,
> bronze of shield,
> emerald of seaweed,
> diamond of dew
> crystal of tear,
> gold of blade,
> garnet of blood.

Seven colour changes as it sang
its seven songs, the Adarna knew
you had landed. And so the golden eggs
and poo you mistook for walnuts
littering the island. Songs of the East:

said to spin the senses — your eyes began
to see a yellow shimmer everywhere.
You even smelled it, this intoxicant
of the blood, lacing the breath
of the king who invited you in.

Your chronicle is studded with it.
I must count the number of times *gold*
appears in your travel bounty that's
neither gold nor silver ... but a book
written with my own hand ...

Presented in 1522 to His Sacred Majesty
Don Carlos, this precious booty
highly esteemed by such a sovereign,
for writers are forever supplicants
to their readers and their reach.

There, too, is empire of the word.
How it expands, how it claims territory,
how it goes to war, how it howls
itself sovereign — then, you heard it sing,
this bird of seven colours seven songs,

and your senses spun, reeled further
to a trail of golden eggs, golden poo
and deeper into dream — then finally
the Piedras Platas, its trunk more silvery
under the moon. And there: the songs of the East,

the final catch, the ultimate. You caught
its eye watching, waiting for you
since the day you landed, and now singing,
singing itself pearl, bronze, emerald, diamond,
crystal, gold, garnet — and your lids

grew heavy, as if the notes had sat on them
and made you see the whole voyage around the world
in a flash, and you knew you have arrived.
So you lay under the tree, under the singing
Adarna finishing its final trill, as you would

finish a book. And the bird flicked its tail
longer than the circumference of the world,
and dropped its dung, turning you to stone.
Sometimes, this is the story of writing:
word not made flesh, but eternal stone.

And we wear it around our necks,
always the weight of what we have written.

QUEEN HUMAMAI'S SOLILOQUY

She was shown an image of our Lady, a very beautiful
wooden child Jesus and a cross. Thereupon, she was overcome
with contrition, and asked for baptism amid her tears.
— Pigafetta, (on the baptism of the heathen queen)

How can these men understand,
my husband included? A child
soon to be taken away from his mother
and left to a stranger? Even if I will love
him dearly, even if there's this piece
of wood, perhaps from a tree
where he was born, to keep him safe
in my care — how his longing
when he sits among my gods at home?
Bereft of his mother, for surely
they'll take the Lady back to the ship,
how his little heart will cry for her and
that tree, that land, that sky of his own home?
But listen: it's all politics, you see,
so I stand by my husband Humabon,
and take this gift of a child: He-Sus,
they call him, like a breath expelled
and its loss sustained with the pucker
of the lips, as if they were about to cry.
For surely they will miss him,
but not as much as a mother will.

How can these men understand,
my husband included? They say,
I must burn all my gods so only
He-Sus will stand in their place.
I see Humabon's face tighten, even
as he whispers to me to nod, nod, nod
in acquiescence (but only for a moment),
as he smiles to this Ca-pi-tan—he-ne-ral
and his slave forever making lines and circles,
lines and circles on pa-pel with a feather.
Making stories, I understand but wonder
how stories can just be lines and circles.
But I take their He-Sus, and swallow back
my tears. It's all politics, you see,
making stories, then making friends:
a barter of wills, a barter of blood.
So Humabon can inspire these pale men
to fight his foe in the other island,
that Lapu-Lapu, that waiting chief
ready now, I'm sure, for the kill.

THE WISDOM TREES

On a morning run

Northbourne we cross, make sure
we do not meet them:
Grandfather and Grandmother
River Peppermint and Brittle Gum.
We step aside, make sure
we don't bump into history and more.

It's not respect but self preservation.
An encounter, a sudden flesh-to-flesh,
would hurt who we think we are
on this ground we have elected
as the birthright of our feet.

Then Macleay: up and down
this street, a stretch of Quercus canopy.
All know colour, wear it with aplomb,
its fickleness, ambiguities
and unrestrained surprises.

Even a leaf may be three colours
all at once. Sure, they know colour
but are colour-blind,
undifferentiating. All tones
gathered under this autumnal shade:

Irish-Aboriginal Stuart in his pram,
six-year old Aluna from Kenya,
and Su with her little koala
made in China, as their mothers
speculate on the latest sale

in children's wear at Target.
But these trees are past speculating.
They know colours bleed
into each other, as they have bled
from old and into this new ground.

Haig Park now, where they hum
when cars whizz past, needles and cones
attuned to traffic. They've perfected
the art of musical transpositions
from the woods of California

to our windswept Capital
on the wheels of government.
There's traffic of trees from north
to south, there's traffic of notes.
Pinus Radiata: their name rings

like a well-worn opera composed
with magpies and cockatoos syncopating
with Hyundais, Toyotas, Fords
and that gleaming Lexus imagining
themselves winged, musical.

Northbourne again: we're returning
from our circuit run. Again,
we skirt past our Grandparents.
But they've always known
we're forever moving on,

composing and recomposing
the earth, and it blurs as we run,
our eyes unseeing, our hearts unwitting,
our feet so soon a-tremor
with a dream brighter

than Lexus: the Light Rail.
Ah, how light our step, how nimble,
except there is this thing
caught in our shoe: a tiny gumnut,
primeval dissident.

THE CONFERENCE OF FEET

And so they came,
all colours, sizes, shapes
and they greeted each other
warmly, assured that
we're all grounded
in good sole company
intimate with earth water air
and their urgencies,
down to our little toes.
After all, this event
is all about what holds us,
the planet, and if it shrugs,
we're done for, feet and all.

And so they came,
walking into the hall:
paa pies voeten fætur
Füße peus 脚 traed
feet pas pedes pieds
chodidla לגר fødder
kājas piedi lábak kal
стопы pés waewae
أقدام bitis vae पद
and so on, and so on,
a passage of multiple hopes,
of gravity — the weight
of the future surely
an emergency — then
they began putting on
their shoes, sandals, boots
and so on, and so on.

They began to notice
which soles were not
leather, and which were not
streamlined to fit,
which were produced where
evoking price tags —
ah, the economics
was just too hard to bear.
And so all walked out.
Of course, everything can wait
until the next conference.

WATER TRAIL

Drought in Legazpi, Philippines

In the house, the taps have dried
I am searching for the water
In the yard, the pump has dried
I am searching for the water
Around the corner, the well has dried
I am searching for the water
Up the hill, the creek has dried

I am eight and it is 38
The path dry as bone
Cracking like my soles — but suddenly
From a distance, flowers
Large as basins and deeply pink
But I am still searching for the water

An hour later
So far away from home
A trickle from a boulder
And a catch in the throat —
An old man shades his sudden tears
From the heat, or me — but I have seen
Tubig, tubig, tubig — water, water, water

HOMESICK FOR CLOUDS

I'm homesick for clouds,
said the river.
If they come,
so would the rain
and I'd flow again.

I'm homesick for clouds,
said the grass.
If they come,
so would the rain
and the river would flow
and I'd be green again.

I'm homesick for clouds,
said the cow.
If they come,
so would the rain
and the river would flow
and the grass would be green
and I'd feed again.

I'm homesick for clouds,
said the woman.
If they come, so would the rain
and the river would flow
and the grass would be green
and the cow would feed
and give me milk again.

I'm homesick for clouds,
said the man soon to be hanged.
If they come, so would the rain
and I'd be a boy again
at the window looking out:
the cow is grazing
on the green paddock
by the flowing river,
and Mother warming
a glass of milk says,
'Now wait till it stops
before you go out and play.'

A LITTLE SCENE

2014: Remembering Legazpi train station

Napupungaw ako.
On the verge of tears
in her pink top and pants
a-swirl with red flowers,
my little sister whispers,

but no one hears.

Napupungaw ako.
A little louder now,
a little more insistent,
and tears almost
fully formed,

still no one hears.

Napupungaw ako
for a train about to leave.
Napupungaw ako
for that trip from home:
Legazpi to Manila.

I hear it now
four decades or so later.
Napupungaw: untranslatable.
Intransitive verb: without an object.
Present tense: it's ongoing

like a train of thought
that never quite arrives
or departs, because the pink
is too pink, the red
too swirly when one remembers.

How does the old train
go again — how the sound
of its heave and sway,
or of a five-year old's
quiet weeping?

How the scene?

I'm almost fifteen,
my brother, twelve,
and we're bursting out of our skin
for summer holiday
in Manila, oh what a dream!

It is time.
Auntie Aden urges
my sister to wave
at father waving
at the window, bereft.

Too much urgings and urgencies.

Like a halo,
loss surrounds him:
three children off
for a month.
Napupungaw ako.

Whose voice then,
whose train of thought,
and what is it about
remembering that leaves
us all bereft?

Recall is loss
turned inside out.
We think we get it back,
that moment
when my sister, only five,

stops our train on its tracks.

*Napupungaw ako
kay Boboy.*
She finds her voice,
she finds the object
of her verb,

our little grammarian.

It's transitive now,
in-transit like her
standing up, tugging
at Auntie's hem,
needing to get off.

I'm homesick for Boboy,
our baby brother left
at home — homesick before
the train leaves the station,
homesick before departure.

Dismayed, my brother and I return
to our skin — it stings
as father, urgently recalled
from his waving post, jumps
on board to rescue

my little sister and her tears.

The train heaves,
pulls out of Legazpi,
pulls out all stops
to this departure — listen
to it sing, we're off, we're off

as our sister becomes a tiny dot beside our father.

Our baby bother
is now forty or so
and none of us three
has seen him
for seven years or so.

Napupungaw ako
for a moment, a memory
of how to miss,
of how to love as unabashedly
as a five-year old.

The train,
oh, the train
of thought, of heart,
this thing that will never arrive
or depart.

TRAIN OF THOUGHT

Wollongong to Sydney

Spectacular is the urge
to stop the train:
to swim with whales
from Austinmer
scale the escarpment
in Coalcliff
jump into the surf
in Stanwell Park
climb the gymeas
in Helensburgh
turn gloriously lilac
as jacarandas
in Kogarah.

And then
the train stops
finally at Central.

Spectacular is the urge
to look away
from the makeshift tents
of the homeless
in Belmore Park
to run and make it
to the station
in time to seek shelter
from the rain.

ON A SLOW TRAIN FROM ALBUQUERQUE

Could be rust, or blood
between boulders as red,
this river coming through.
She thinks of age, of hurt,
how sharp the edge,
how deep the drop.
And how sudden
this rain,
the sun stolen
(too quickly before she can shield her eyes).
The river too, by rocks as high as God.
Now the window's streaked,
first drops like salvation.
Not in the forecast.
Just sneaks up on you,
the edge, the drop,
rust blood river
again
behind those junipers.
And then
again
the sun.

OUTBOUND

For Blind Willie Johnson
Dark Was the Night, Cold Was the Ground on the *Voyager*

Perhaps it's all in the slide out and back
or in the hum to moan to cry to wail to hum
circumnavigating the universe
of muscle, bone and always
a vibrato of corpuscles
as we go further out, out with you sliding into
mourning into supplication into exaltation
into mourning again
in search of a kinder sun
and half believe out there
your mmm aaah aaay ooo mmm
hits some lonely asteroid
slides into it, vibrates it, wakes its
corpuscles to jam with you
even when all your crying has ended
for when dark is the night, cold is the ground
there will always be more crying yet
so we hum moan cry wail hum, slide further out
expanding hum within the humming of a further universe
in all variations, all gradations of dark and light
for there too is lightness in your throat, lips
in the chiaroscuro of your fingers
sliding from fret to fret, away and back, away and back
circumnavigating a wish to go outbound and return
even as we dally in all directions, high, low, sideways
to left, right, to paths unimagined
improvising what it means
to hum moan cry wail hum

what it means
to be human
but sometimes
there's a knock of steel on wood
catching us by surprise
as if your knuckle just knocked us off our perch
on a high note we think we know by now
(economics and politics, affairs more loved than love)
but never ever knew and always wish to know
before we slide past ourselves again
corpuscles vibrating but catching
only darkness
and a chill
still asking
do we know any better
do we see any clearer?

STAR, NOTE, TREE

For Pauline Hopkins
who restored the stars

It was 2004
when the stars went out
when I began

my long walk
with Amedea.
I kept walking,

kept spinning
light, song, life:
a star, a note, a tree

as compass
like the locust on her brow
taking her beyond the border

where I was made
strange to what I've spun,
taken by two girls

(I've met only
in a dream)
by the hand.

Once in a while,
the three of us
looked up

to check the holes
up there and wondered
how to repair them.

Then 2015:
the girls reached
their journey's end

and I was left
alone at the border
still checking the sky.

In the middle
of a desert (I only ever
dreamt about),

you tapped me
on the shoulder
weighed with wonder.

Dear reader-dreamer,
you said, *Listen,*
it's a symphony

you've spun —
you held my hand
and at the border

we closed our eyes
to listen better
together, listen

to trees sprouting,
the desert greening,
to light returning,

ever more brilliant,
and finding their own
places in the sky.

PASSAGE

O Mary like a queen
born in Dundee
greets me at a corridor
in Wollongong.

The open arms and smile
sweep me off my feet.
It's 14 February 1991
and she's my Valentine.

I'm a hungry Filipino student
just landed in Australia
and at International House,
it's way past lunch,

but she is resolute,
calling out to the chef,
Make this young woman
a sandwich, please.

So, my first meal in Australia:
sitting with Queen Mary
patching a tea towel,
regaled by her stories of the city
that becomes my home for 24 years.

*

Then, Grandmother
in the bus disarms me
on my first month
in this city by the sea.

I'm missing home,
also a city between
a mountain
and the sea —

so when
I board a bus and
lose my footing
and Grandmother

(or this is how to me
she suddenly becomes)
leans forward and asks,
You'right, love?

I'm righted, once again
on solid ground.
No common slang for me
steadying my feet,

my heart, but an endearment
meant for me alone.
So unabashedly, there and then,
I own it: Love.

*

And May also from Dundee
and Scottish to the bone,
another queen (of treacle scones)
becomes my next-door neighbour.

In a flat on my 9th month or so,
she takes charge
of my homesickness
with her Scottish brogue

155

early on comprehensible
(to my awkward ear)
only as singing — a trill,
a thrill of notes,

their ascensions and declensions
hinged to the tone of the tale
of her 12-year old succulent
spilling like a green tail

all the way to the floor
from the pot on the top shelf
where her eldest son lives:
a handsome picture, still smiling

long after — her brogue dips
and dives — *Mothers should never
outlive their sons* —
and we grow as silent as our cups.

*

Years later, the boy at the rock pool
perhaps has known it all along
when he meets the non-swimmer.
Around nine and strokes

sure and brave unlike mine,
thirty-six and drowning in
my dark flat, dark thoughts
for a year, unable to surface

for air. Only the water
and the swimming lessons
keep me trying, stroke
by stroke, how to breathe

again and live. So yes,
he's known it all along,
old in his swimming bones,
when the non-swimmer

stops in the middle
of the pool, flailing, gasping,
I lost my strokes,
and assuredly

he throws out an arm
and his nine-year old wisdom:
Hold my hand
and we'll swim together.

*

So here I am alive
after a passage of salvations,
remembering that
kindness is a passage too

from bank to bank
and the water may be deep,
unplumbed, even treacherous
and sometimes we lose our strokes.

Yet we make the crossing,
meet each other in the deepest part
and trust the old refrain: Hold my hand
and we'll swim together.

HOMECOMING

For Cindy, Yueying and Chunfeng

All blocked: nose, head, throat,
a bad cold here to wreck the poet's
dreams, but Cindy at reception makes her
the sweetest ginger tea and clears
the passages for a word, a line, then another
as if dreams could rise from a steaming cup.

The poet thinks of Grandmother,
her secret about ginger, this little
yellow root, gold unearthed from her garden
in another country where she told
the story of how her Chinese father
left when she was in the womb

and her dream of meeting him,
making him some golden tea
to clear a passage in the heart,
and the poet thought maybe
his cold lasted forever, Grandmother's
dream only a dream until she died.

Later, the poet is eating leftover
sweet potatoes from breakfast,
and Cindy knocks at her door,
a quiet rap: *Would you like to eat
lunch with us in kitchen?*
The poet's heart becomes the passage

suddenly, for Great-grandfather
to come home: China coming
through in this surprise, this kindness
of new friends: Cindy, Yueying, Chunfeng
sitting her down and her bad cold
and no Chinese at all except, *Xie xie* —

thank you — she's beside herself
with gratitude, the three women
all smiles and little English, but Cindy is on
her iPhone, finding the words, lines
to translate for Yueying, who cleans
the rooms each day, for Chunfeng who cooks

the breakfast for poets, because
dreams pass better through a full
stomach. The poet tells them her Great-
grandfather is Chinese, but how
to tell the full story, its nuances
and how Great-grandfather has come home

now, here, at the table even
with no Chinese and little English,
for the poem passes in the arc
of a gesture completed in a smile
and the language of sipping egg
and tomato soup together, warm, so warm.

THIS IS THE MAN

For Reinis

This is the man I love
caught between sky
and earth — and histories
and homes.

A Hopi house, a canyon grand enough to last us a lifetime
and a dream.

This is the man I love
tucked between desert scrub and the cares that come
with an impending storm. One may read it
in the sky, just as he reads the sign:

The houses of the Hopi are used for shelter, work, storage and ceremonial
practices ... The clay is used to connect the structural elements.
This building technique allowed the Hopi to disassemble or expand
upon the existing structure.

How were the Hopi disassembled
by the storm of Spanish conquistadores or
of White America, before and after they were United?

This is the man I love
born in Riga, Latvia
stormed by the Germans, then the Russians
and at two years old in World War II,
on a surgeon's table
with his mother reassembling
her heart, his home —
later, at six,
a refugee camp in Oldenburg,
at eight,
a migrant camp in Bathurst, Australia.

On and beyond these histories, how do we expand existence —
yours, mine, his, the Hopi's?

Burrowed among the roots
of the desert scrub
and disassembling-reassembling hearts
before and now
is a scorpion,
the sting
of provenance:
where we came from, how we got here.

We who look at these —
the Hopi house, the canyon grand,
the man I love —
we do not feel the sting.
Or the urge
of the bud of a bud.
Will it be a yellow flower
like a desert star
disassembling a storm?
Or a pink cup
small enough to tuck into a heart
yet large enough to hold
our histories combined?

This is the man I love:
look with him
look into him
and read the signs

not just of storms weathered
or storms heralded
but of the burrowed life.

BETWEEN COOK AND AMIRA

Always there are storms
in the open sea,
the equaliser.

All yearn for land:
Magellan, Cook, Columbus,
Phuong, Badri, Amira

leaving home and country,
a wife, a son, a garden,
those flowers, that bed.

Listen to them dream
in the same boat.
Take their pulse,

a hope murmur
in the wrist,
now a tempest

as the craft careens —
but suddenly, land!
O gratitude, O joy.

Magellan, Cook, Columbus
praise their god
and check their maps,

their men, their arms,
the shore for natives —
there could be accidents.

Phuong, Badri, Amira
praise their god,
and check their children,

the shore for any living soul —
there could be accidents
of kindness here.

MIGRATIONS

When leatherbacks stop
foraging off the coast of California
then mating en route to Oahu
transiting through West Papua
and nesting in Bundaberg.
When whales stop
their great sonar voyages.
When arctic terns stop
circumnavigating the globe
in a tireless embrace.
When caribous stop
their epic trek season after season.
When monarch butterflies stop
turning the sky ochre
through 3000 miles.

Because water, air, land
have sprouted elemental barricades
no flipper, fin, tail, or wing
can cross,

then we can stop the boats,
stop the urge to feed, to mate, to nest,
stop the wish to greet
a kinder sun.

LOVE IS PLANETARY

from the first urge,
no, from the inkling
of an urge — perhaps
way before time
before the big bang
when black holes,
matter and antimatter
and space were yet
light years unknown
to each other.

This is the astronomy
of our chance to meet
even with the most
strange, most distant
and evolve
by accident something
even stranger:
a ringed planet,
a newborn star
or this thing
called earth.

So sweetheart
from the other side
of the globe, ocean,
river, field, mountain,
wall, barbed wire or
the border of tanks and guns,
faceless yet to each other
there is hope for us.

BECAUSE: AN AFTERWORD

Let the poem speak for itself. No poet must explain. Do not betray the labour. Yet I choose to reveal the accidents, the gifts behind this book.

It began on the 18 October 2014 in a tourist bus across the desert, after visiting the Grand Canyon. As we sped along, behind the glass window was a black bird close to an eerie sun, like a white hole against storm grey sky. I took a picture: an accident of composition. A poem.

As Reinis and I travelled south, more images composed and recomposed me into seeing the world anew. So, more poems. Then in Australia and later on a trip to Spain, China, Philippines and while revisiting old photos and poetry scribbles, memories, dreams, histories and stories told me once, each time something else was revealed. I began seeing images as if for the first time. As if this tree, this rock, this light was the only tree, rock, light in the planet. Seeing was like a beautiful accident. A flash behind the eyes, a quick poem. Something else was happening. So I returned to the poetry book after four novels.

I am awed, grateful. Especially for the greater gifts from this something else, the accidents of kindness and insight in their passage through my life. Thank you, Lucy, Fan, Cassandra, Yanfen and Guanwen, Banduk, Jenni, Brian and Belinda, Ian, Denmark, Encarni, Fernando, Javier and Magdalena, Leila, Yueying, Chunfeng and Cindy; Mary, May, grandmother in the bus, boy at the rock pool; Pauline, Susan, Renate and the women of the volcano: Marlene, Gloria, Phoebe, Maricel; Elaine and all the students of Sun Yat-sen University; the ghosts of Lorca, Dickinson, Rumi, Rilke, Keats, Willie Johnson, and John Lennon; the desaparecidos and all those crossing the border to find a home, they who must not disappear from our hope of a kinder sun; Amedea, Stephanus, Fortunata, Seruilius and their descendants; the father and son Chen from Dawan; even Pigafetta, Magellan and Beatriz, Cook and Elizabeth, Humabon, Humamai and Lapu-Lapu; and most especially Reinis, Rolando, Lea, Noel, Amparo, Nicolas, Mama Ola, my lost Chinese great-grandfather, and everyone who touched me into seeing, into being, including the leatherback, terns and monarch butterflies, the caribous and dragons, the grazing calf and bookstore cats, the wisdom trees and flowers, mountains and clouds, desert, rocks and rivers, the silent stones and singing birds; Legazpi, Wollongong, Canberra, Arizona, Albuquerque, Granada, Seville, Córdoba, Yangshuo, Guangzhou and Jiangmen; the Grand Canyon, Blue Mountains, Mayon volcano and karst mountains; and all the other tongues sneaking into the English language now — but they have always been there, even before my English grown in the Philippines and growing into something else in Australia.

Perhaps this is the poem. This something else.

Merlinda Bobis
5 February 2017

APPENDIX: GLOSSARY AND REFERENCES

Glossary

Bacalhau com natas. Portuguese dish: salted cod baked in cream. Salted cod: referred to as 'fiel amigo' (faithful friend) of Portuguese cuisine.

Cataplana de marisco. Portuguese seafood dish cooked in a cataplana, a copper cooking dish.

Ferdinand Magellan (as he is known in the English-speaking world). Explorer and navigator whose expedition (1519–1522) is said to be the first to circumnavigate the globe; there are historical controversies on who was 'first'. A Portuguese (Fernão de Magalhães) of noble lineage, as a boy he served as Page for then Queen Leonora. In her Court he studied navigation, astronomy and cartography. In 1507 he explored the Malaccas (Malaysia) and might have sailed as far as the Moluccas (Indonesia), the Spice Islands, the original source of the most valuable spices like cloves and nutmeg. In 1517 he moved to Spain (Fernando de Magallanes) where King Charles I (later Charles V of the Holy Roman Empire) supported his expedition that led to the circumnavigation of the globe. He travelled with the Italian chronicler, Antonio Pigafetta, who documented the expedition and wrote the book *Magellan's Voyage Around the Globe*. In 1521 Magellan arrived in Homonhon (one of the Philippine islands), which he claimed for Spain. He was killed in Mactan by the warrior Datu Lapu-Lapu. Magellan's is a journey of exploration, conquest, and, in some respect, also of identity (and names): from Portuguese, to Spanish, to the famous navigator to the New World, as he is now known. See: <http://www.history.com/topics/exploration/ferdinand-magellan> and <http://www.philippine-history.org/spanish-expeditions.htm>

Padre Nuestro Que Estás en Los Cielos. Our Father who art in heaven ('Lord's Prayer').

Palago. Yellow-vented bulbul, Philippine bird.

Silencio ahora, queridos, y escuchan, escuchan. Silence now, dearests, and listen, listen. (Lullaby composed by M. Bobis).

Sopa de lentilha. Lentil soup.

Tagbaya. Baya Weaver (Ploceus philippinus infortunatus), Philippine bird.

Waling-waling. Vanda Sanderiana known as 'Queen of Philippine Orchids.'

References

Blake, William, 'The Tiger' in *The College Survey of English Literature*. General Ed. Alexander M. Witherspoon. New York & Burlingame: Harcourt, Brace & World, Inc., 1951, p.#667. ('Tiger! Tiger! burning bright / In the forests of the night, / What immortal hand or eye / Could frame thy fearful symmetry?')

Navarro Chueca, Javier. Alfacar excavation, Granada, Spain, 1 October 2016. (Javier tells the story of the sister waiting to confirm that the unearthed skull is 'mi hermana', my sister, as Encarnacion Hidalgo Tenorio translates. It is alleged that Lorca was shot in Alfacar.) See: <http://www.typicallyspanish.com/news-spain/granada/Archaeologists_face_today_the_last_phase_in_the_search_for_Lorca_s_grave.shtml> and <http://progressive.org/magazine/retrieving-bones-reviving-memories-the-practice-of-reconcili/>

Classics Museum, The Australian National University. Visited 26 April 2016. (Funerary relic [1st or 2nd Century AD]: 'To the departed spirit of M. Seruilius Gemellus, who lived 9 years, 2 months and 27 days: set up by his parents Stephanus and Fortunata for their dutiful son and for themselves and for their [?] descendants — ')

Cook, James, 'Captain Cook's Journal' in *First Voyage Round the World Made in H.M. Bark 'Endeavour' 1768-71*. London: Elliot Stock, 1893. Project Gutenberg Australia. <http://gutenberg.net.au/ebooks/e00043.html> Accessed 8 August 2016. ('The String of Beads, etc., we had left with the Children last night were found laying in the Hutts this morning; probably the Natives were afraid to take them away.' [p. #50] 'Their features were far from being disagreeable; their Voices were soft and tunable, and they could easily repeat any word after us.' [p. #56])

Dickinson, Emily, letter to Thomas Wentworth Higginson about 1870. In *Selected Poems of Emily Dickinson*. Ed, James Reeves, with introduction and notes. London: Heinemann, 1959, p.#140. See also *Letters of Emily Dickinson*. Eds. Thomas H. Johnson and Theodora Ward. Cambridge: Harvard University Press, 1958. ('If I read a book and it makes my whole body so cold no fire can ever warm me, I know that is poetry. If I feel physically as if the top of my head were taken off, I know that is poetry. These are the only ways I know it. Is there any other way?')

Garcia Lorca, Federico, 'Romance Sonámbulo' in *Lorca Selected Poems*. Trans. J. L. Gili. Middlesex, England: Penguin Books, 1960, pp.#39–42. ('Verde que te quiero verde.': 'Green, green, I love you green.' 'Con la sombre en la cintura / ella sigue en su baranda, / verde carne, pelo verde …': With the shadow at her waist she dreams on her balcony, green flesh, green hair …' '… and the mountain, like a thieving cat, bristles its sour agaves.' 'The full wind left in the mouth a strange taste of gall, of mint, and of sweet-basil.' 'How often, she would wait for you, cool face, black hair, on this green balustrade!')

Gentle, Ian, in a conversation, University of Wollongong, September 2010. ('It's a squig, that sudden movement in the undergrowth.')

Holland, Rupert S., *Historic Ships*. Bremen: Erscheinungsjahr, maritimepress, 2012, p.#146. ('Magellan had fallen in April, 1521; in September of that same year his little son Rodrigo dies, and by March, 1522 Magellan's wife Beatiz had learned from the Portuguese Indies of the fate of her husband.')

Leila, interview at As-Sirat, Moroccan café, Granada, Spain, 9 September 2006. (La Pena Negra: '… is "the black pity" … if you're not fighting, he can swallow you.')

Mason, Moya K., 'Ancient Roman Women. A Look at Their Lives.' <http://www.moyak.com/papers/roman-women.html> Accessed 16 February 2017. ('Girls married very young. Many died in childbirth or because they were weakened from having too many children without reprieve. A funerary inscription to a woman named Veturia provides a good example of this: she was married at eleven, gave birth to six children, and died at twenty-seven.')

Merin, Cassandra Fate B., Drawing made at Cabalawan Transitional Shelter, Tacloban, Philippines, 28 October 2015. (With her text naming her wish — 'Gusto ko sama-sama kaming pamilya.' [I wish we were together as a family.] — and identifying various spaces and characters in her drawing.)

'Mrs. Cook's Valentine's Day', *Australian National Maritime Museum*, 2013. <https://anmm.wordpress.com/2013/02/14/mrs-cooks-valentines-day/> Last accessed 16 February 2017 ('She also kept a small, coffin-shaped, wooden "ditty box" which held a tiny painting of Cook's death and a lock of his hair.')

Museo Arqueológico de Córdoba, Spain. Visited 9 October 2016. ('Lucerna. Lamp. Romana. Siglo 1.' 'Fragmento de sarcófago con ¿magistrados? Fragment of sarcophagus depicting magistrates (?). Paleocristiano, Siglo IV')

Native American Village (signage), Grand Canyon (West). Visited 18 October 2014. See also: <http://www.iltm.com/__novadocuments/ 117606?v=635997954900400000> ('The houses of the Hopi are used for shelter, work, storage and ceremonial practices. The distinguishing characteristic of the Hopi building is the stonework. The stone and mortar is coated with plaster and painted with whitewash. The clay is used to connect the structural elements. This building technique allowed the Hopi to disassemble or expand upon the existing structure.')

Pigafetta, Antonio, *Magellan's Voyage Around the Globe*. Trans. James Alexander Robertson. Cleveland: The Arthur H. Clark Company, 1906. ('He gave them many knives, scissors, mirrors, bells, and glass beads; and those two having their hands filled with the said articles, the captain-general had two pairs of manacles brought, such as are fastened on the feet.' [p.#56] 'The fish [that hunt] are of three sorts, and are one braza and more in length, and are called dorado, albicore, and bonito. Those fish follow the flying fish called colondrini, which are one palmo and more in length and very good to eat. When the above three kinds [of fish] find any of those flying fish, the latter immediately leap from the water and fly as long as their wings are wet — more than a crossbow's flight. While they are flying, the others run along back of them under the water following the shadow of the flying fish. The latter have no sooner fallen into the water than the others immediately seize and eat them. It is in fine a very amusing thing to watch.' [p.#73] 'The captain-general wished to stop at the large island and get some fresh food, but he was unable to do so because the inhabitants of that island entered the ships and stole whatever the could lay their hands on, so that we could not protect ourselves.' [p.#91] 'When we wounded any of those people with our crossbow shafts, which passed completely through their loins from one side to the other, they, looking at it, pulled on the shaft now on this and now on that side, and then drew it out, with great astonishment, and so died; others who were wounded in the breast did the same, which moved us to great compassion. [...] We saw some women in their boats who were crying out and tearing their hair, for love, I believe, of their dead.' [p.#93] 'Pieces of gold, of the size of walnuts and eggs are found by sifting the earth in the island of that king who came to our ships. All the dishes of that king are gold and also some portion of his house, as we were told by that king himself.' [pp.#118–119] 'They played so harmoniously that one would believe they possessed good musical sense. Those girls were very beautiful and almost as white as our girls and as large.' [p.#146–147] 'She was shown an image of our Lady, a very beautiful wooden child Jesus and a cross. Thereupon, she was overcome with contrition, and asked for baptism amid her tears.' [p.#155] '... I presented to his sacred Majesty, Don Carlo, neither gold nor silver, but things very highly esteemed by such a sovereign. Among other things I gave him a book, written by my hand, concerning all the matters that had occurred from day to day during our voyage.' [p.#189])

Rigsby, Michael, 'Not just a red fluid, blood is a marvel of complexity' in *Yale Health Care*, Vol IX No. 6, Nov–Dec 2006, p.#1. ('Blood courses through our language.')

Rilke, Rainer Maria, 'The Panther' in *The Selected Poetry of Rainer Maria Rilke*. Ed. & Trans. Stephen Mitchell. New York: Vintage International, 1989, p.#25. ('Only at certain times, the curtain of the pupils/lifts, quietly—. An image enters in,/rushes down through the tensed, arrested muscles, /plunges into the heart and is gone.' 'As he paces in cramped circles, over and over,/the movement of his powerful soft strides/is like a ritual dance around a center/in which a mighty will stands paralyzed.')

Rumi, Jelaluddin, 'Only Breath' in *The Essential Rumi*. Trans. Coleman Barks with John Moyne. San Francisco: Harper Collins, 1995, p.#32. ('Not Christian or Jew or Muslim, not Hindu,/Buddhist, sufi, or zen. Not any religion/or cultural system ...' 'I belong to the beloved, have seen the two /worlds as one and that one call to and know,/first, last, outer, inner, only that/breath breathing human being.')

Ukrainian Holodomor Memorial, Turner, Canberra ACT. Visited 13 June 2016. See also: <https://www.youtube.com/watch?v=fEgPr8M2ftk> ('Execution by Hunger 1932–1933. '... a man-made famine claimed the lives of more than 7,000,000 men, women and children in Ukraine. This enforced famine-genocide was perpetrated by the regime of the Communist Party of the U.S.S.R. as a consequence of the resistance of the Ukrainian nation to Russian occupation ...')

'Story behind Qiaopi: A Case Study of Toponymy', Provincial Archives of Canton, Guangzhou, 18 October 2016, p.#3. Trans. Li, Peiyi. Accessed 8 November 2016. <http://mp.weixin.qq.com/s?__biz=MzI1 NTI5MzYyNA==&mid=2247484352&idx=1&sn=bf552e4c6afc721 fdf57f08312237c6d&chksm=ea396217dd4eeb0193947e8397cad 14f52dade9ba313457d033a21098eaeee675bf8ede98c9b&mpshare= 1&scene=1&srcid=1109KO6IiaSHTN0zPgDSs6MB&from=single message&isappinstalled=0#wechat_redirect> ('This letter contains eight pounds in total. Please forward it to my son CHEN Rongbai in Dawan Village from CHEN Songke, NEW GOLD MOUNTAIN [Chinese name for Melbourne].')

Walker, Hugh Dyson, *East Asia: A New History*. Bloomington: Author House, 2012, p.#256. ('Brought to China from Iran, cobalt was called Huiqing, Muslim Blue.')